On the Mesa
An Anthology of Bolinas Writing

Edited by Joel Weishaus
50th Anniversary Edition edited by Ben Estes
Afterword by Lytle Shaw

To Jim — with gratitude for the gift of poetry, which has enriched my life — Kate 8/22

The Song Cave

Contents

Preface

In celebration of the 50th anniversary of *On the Mesa: An Anthology of Bolinas Writers*, I am excited to present this expanded edition that includes more than 65 new poems by 19 more authors who were in this geographical area around the time of its publication. Originally published in 1971 by City Lights Books and edited by Joel Weishaus, the additions I have made to the anthology double the number of writers found in the original volume. Whenever adding a new author, or choosing which of their poems to include, I tried to stay as true as possible to the casually esoteric yet reverent nature of the original volume in capturing this wobbly point of time in the United States in 1971: Richard Nixon is the President, thousands are still protesting the war in Viet Nam, Charles Manson has just been given the death sentence in prison, unemployment rates across the country are rapidly spiking, the U.S. dollar's value is plummeting, The Weather Underground has set off bombs in Washington D.C., *A Clockwork Orange* and *The Last Picture Show* are playing in the movie theaters, and Disney World has just opened in Orlando, Florida.

My initial interest in putting together a new edition of this anthology stems from my love of the original version: the counterculture literary puzzle that this very specific place in time stands for, a refuge for San Francisco Renaissance and Beat poets and prominent poets of the New York School and Black Mountain College all living and working together, in one place, for a brief period of time. But just as important, half a century later, is how relevant all of the work still feels. I find familiar their impulse for a simpler way of life. If not simpler, then easier, quieter. If not easier or quieter, at least one that feels closer to what might be in line with one's natural rhythms, where internal reflection may not need to be the chore it sometimes feels it can be living in a crowded urban area. Maybe too it is about reassessing one's place in a world that feels extremely illogical. It's an impulse that I think a lot of us are feeling now. Today, typing this up 24 hours before the election of 2020, eight months into a global pandemic and endless streams of governmental lying and corporate corruption, there has been a worldwide reassessment of *What is important?* Followed quickly with *What do I hold most dear?* Clean air. Water. Oceans. Forests. Clearly defined personal space. Friendly communal spaces. The protection of wild animals. Faith. Having work that feels important. Food. Friends. Again, love. Magic. Human touch. Finding a place and a community where one feels safe and can create. We can see all of these things being reconsidered by the writers in *On the Mesa*.

By no means is this version of the Bolinas story definitive. It exists here as one collection of material, out of which hundreds of other different groupings could be made from the work of the writers and artists who felt drawn to this willfully hidden Brigadoon on the California coast, whose natural measures and tides can be felt in each of the poems.

Many thanks to Anne Waldman and Lewis Warsh for being the sounding board for my first thoughts on this project, and also the kind generosity of Alice Notley, Duncan McNaughton, each of the authors and their families, and to Lytle Shaw, Gerard Malanga, Cedar Sigo, Kevin Opstedal, Nick Sturm, and of course Joel Weishaus.

—BEN ESTES

MICHAEL BOND

The Moon of Black Cherries

Wishing to be more than I am
or other than I am
or being not complete with the living
that is now mine
being afraid that I am not completely
doing what I am
is crazy now
and always was
and always will be
is
such verbs, such verbs as these
where shall I beguile myself to?
words what words make the difference
between being and being not?

corralled by my ideas I have seen a horse
follow me through a field of grass
without stopping to eat because I
held before her nose a handful of dried weeds

everything that I can learn, the man with his mind
can learn, must first have been unlearned
once before, in the journey from the prairie
to the city

the most advanced of minds
is only best
at doing with a machine the tasks
the heart was once at home with

I feel tired and dissolute
the cries of children arguing distract me
I think of Yellowstone
of grizzlies
and dusk
a famine of the heart
is what we know
not only the prisoners of 2nd Avenue
but also we who bring our city minds
to the grasslands

there are images that pin my heart
to circumstance
unknown,
blood spurts from the past
release me
grandfathers
spirits
ask me what I am doing
with my hands posed before this typewriter this machine
in adoration? no—simply in ineffectiveness

living in smoke, we are haunted by a dream,
by shapes moving through the cloud
painted warriors riding in and out
we would be them we say

we have not even a candle
hungry for a truth, any truth
we have no clothes
no horses
and there is no land left
to travel on
there is truly nowhere left
to go—
is this the truth
we seek?

last night I had a dream
I have had so many
I was on my pony
riding north and east
each day was new
the land unending
I could have travelled for
ever
had I wanted

each day grass
           for the pony
water
           cool to drink
game
           to ease my hunger
and skins
           of antelope
and deer
           and bison

and elk
        and all the four
footed creatures of this earth
beside me
"Where are you going little one,"
the grandfathers asked me
"I am going to the hills, O Great Ones,

"I am going to the hills, the Black
Hills, to dance with my enemies the Crows,
under the waxing light of the moon,
the Moon of Black Cherries, under the
yellow moon"

for all that has been before shall be again
all that was is now and always will
there is nothing that lies forgotten under the grass
our dead shall be avenged
for the victors die of poison
and our dead, grandfathers, our ancestors, have feet of grass,
bones of air

skin of clear stream water
with their sharp eyes they watch me

Scorpio Among the Apple Trees

It is Scorpio among the apple trees.
Between the aisles that line
the present and the past
bare fruit is fallen
caught in webs of grass,
the earth shall eat them.

It is a time of passion, a time
of plenty, the earth turns fiercely over,
a time of winter coming
and hunger under apple bark.
Cicadas sing an empty song.
I too have stopped, sit hungrily
among the apple trees.

Out of passion in a time
of plenty let the gods deliver me,
let me no longer seek a way
in no way,
let the warmth of death
like sugar in a coffee spoon
teach me the folly
of the dream
undreamt.

This dream a road that men
and women travel on.
The sun washed their feet.

They have taken off their fears and carry them slung
over one shoulder.
In the heat of the day,
in the remembrance of the death,
they lay them down, these burdens,
and walk on.

The men the women stop.
They plant corn and build houses.
The sparrows of the fields fly into their windows
        and break their necks
on invisible panes of glass,
and fall to lie invisibly in the tall grass,
heads ajar, feet slightly curled.

And so fear fades before acceptance as a traveler leaves the highway
        to sleep in the fields.
Time turns, a stone,
the dream grows in waking.
There is no answer to carry men
        like camionettes
along the highways of the soul.
Time holds no place to build
        such dwellings.
as the body hungers after.

We the dreamers soon lie naked
        in our dream
within the naked fields.
We break our necks on invisible panes
of worlds that hold us

tightly clasped
like stones inside a mountain.
The sun in passing turns us into grass
that sparrows eat;
our heartbeat joins the stars,
the faraway stars in the great fields
        of night,
leaves in the great dwelling place
        beyond the sun,
the stars that break on invisible paths
        of light,
to fall invisibly into time,
heads ajar, feet slightly curled.

DAVID MELTZER

Songs of David Dog the Lion

1.
David Dog the Lion in canyon country sees
green, white, yellow, sees
blue sky prism-dome, sees
only what she springs forth as song,
as thought, as sunlight works out
new code for further spec.
David Dog the Lion
sees only what he's seen before
but now anew as if awakened.
Shakes the mountain off.
Hurt his head so
for so long O
so long, city, goodbye.
Dogs barking up & down the hills,
the rocky roads,
day & night. So long, city,
goodbye, says David Dog the Lion,
dreamer sitting on the top branch of
the local redwood castle.

2.
David Dog the Lion
lord of his shadow's creeping lair.
Each step a snapshot of hell on earth.
Non-stop genocide.
His blue sneakers break grass stalks,
squash a squad of ants
O God the consequences of being
attached to infinity.
Rude, constant intruder,
David Dog the Lion,
a fatal galaxy,
thumbs a ride into town.

3.
Eye imposition. I
know what I know, what I can
lay my hands on, touch,
pull from earth, make my own,
own what I know by my eye's grasp of it.
I know what I want.
I got my eye on it.
The eyes have it.
The eye an earth in space. A part.
apart, from the invention of a nest.
walls to hold it all inside of
as hide holds it all inside of
earth holds it all inside of a fiery core,
alchemic sun the eye can't look at too long
without being shut off, making walls
to hold dark inside of, hide

the swallowed light, snuffed-out like
candlelight.
In sight of stars poets tell us:
holes heavenly light shines thru,
holes angels peek thru to see what they can see
thru eyes that are stars & earths & suns in space,
points of light

                    the sound of her dance,
earth's song, roars like lions.
Her veils webbed with Shasta daisies.
David Dog the Lion lays
stoned-out on a burial mound
crowned with seashells.
This place made magic
by Marin tribesmen
who once hunted herbs & wild deer.
Long before the eye grew large.
Down below the land grows A-frame tipis
white moon-faced machinists live in,
warming themselves before neon fire.

4.
David Dog the Lion
stalks an earthmover tire
which fell down the falls
to land in mud at stream's end, jammed
into the sewer's round mouth,
a clay tunnel larded with a day's debris.
Cans bottles, aluminum barbecue foil,
leaves, cones, branches

steel wool, dead animals, bent fenders, rags, jars,
uncertain times mulched,
a child's red sneaker.

•

The Vision of the Moment at Stream's End

Soon platforms above earth will house machines to manufacture more
endless duplication of
stuff & death
garbage
        floats by in a serene silence
        blocks-out starlight
        shining thru the gas
surrounding us.

From: Sefer Ha-Adam

Life's round
holds us to the deer dance
along cave walls of Lascaux
O makers hand!
Man zoos all the moves,
that is possessed by life,
propelled by energy art traps
but cannot see.
Begin again. Faith is the same.
One to one. One to One.
Aleph. Tav. All of us.
Prepare Eden's green bed & sleep together
beneath a code of stars whose pulse
parts secret veils as we lay
watching the heavens
watch us
held in life's round.

•

Our treehouse green with spring light.
Impossible to tell you how green breaks sunrays
thru ancient redwood hair.
Light bends into webs of cool shade falling
on pine needles
large leaf
bright red mushroom domes
mustard colored slugs freckled dark-brown
mulch

the soft step
her breath
Noon light off popcorn cherryblossom boughs.
Skier light
racing down a bright slope.

•

It's the springing forth of the new black bugs
beetles with crisp blue shells
sinister spiders crawl from folklore
neon-red triangle bottoms
the light speaks thru new-hatched insect ciphers
grey turned white potato bugs
dry husks of death in the spiderweb
tremble to my breath, a music

It's the springing forth of green buds
uncurling like tongue from stems
shooting forth from venerable cacti
lined along the windowledge

The springing forth of cosmic bulbs
blue tint to purple red
well-hung fuchsias soon full-bloomed

It's a green uprising of weed & clover
grass spears reaching higher each season
out of ground we tried to till but found
useless for want of constant sunlight
The light speaks thru green leaves
thin membrane makes yellow shadows on the earth

MAX CROSLEY

Epic Today

A black and ochre-fuzzed bee hovers and lands on the flower
of a weed I'm out of the house, down to the end of the road. Having
paid my dues, I now live and work in an unurban world where the
bees continue to collect pollen and I can make all the world honey I
try, here, now, on this path, down the cliffs off the mesa, to the sea,
no more imaginary mountains, imaginary seas . . . on the edge of
a country I once knew had no edge . . . yellow daisy weeds . . . the
grandeur . . . now feeling . . . seeing myself from there (10 years) to
here . . . to live in a place that is always spring . . . Some flowers hang
on the bushes here all year long . . . didn't shave today . . . many flying
black multi-sized bugs down the zig-zag tunneled path . . . the sea
keeping a locomotive pace to its waves, rushing and breaking in . . .
ankle still aches from the sprain . . . pause, rest here.

Poochie, our dog, comes back from running the deer through
the small willows that grow down these hills to the shore, breathless,
ready for me to get up and follow her down the path. I used to go
out like this and get swirling-ass drunk and write into drunken
confusion . . . sneaking out from under a pile-driver of a society of job
which was all the same then . . . now I go out at my own bidding . . .
as welfare . . . smoke a puff or two of my pipe and with much time and
crystal clarity I sit here on this path and react with where I am and how
it hits me . . . how much time the wind has. I eat a blackberry. Poochie
comes back from hunting really anxious to go this time. I get up and
walk under ivy, eat another berry. The paranoia of being middle-age

and care-too-much diminishes to simple joy and the parade of vision . . .
the three-foot horsetail plants, fallen hemlock covered path . . . nature
thickens as the line from this felt tip pen . . . change to ball point . . .
fight on and free . . .

The dirt path of crumbled sediment rock . . . faint traces of
other scuffs of shoes . . . sound of crickets and above all the waves . . .
ceaseless, relentless, wearing away this edge of a country, stagger,
crush—flow and break . . . sounds of THE mother rocking . . . it grows
cooler, near the water . . . Horse dung on the path . . . many feeling
stretches of vine reaching out for an unknown clench of barrier to the
sea . . . I eat more berries — (Poochie eats grasshoppers) . . . eat em by
the hours . . . finally right, deliciously black, prickly stemmed, fought,
scratched for . . . wind into the vines . . . to eat and pass on.

Now on the beach to walk pass on . . . the tides in on the
beach diminished . . . White foam up to my feet as I pause to write . . .
it just keeps coming . . . ankle bent on the rocks . . . the cliffs falling . . .
it keeps coming with its dirty angry waste shaped motion . . . hear the
birds faintly . . . but here, always the rhythm to keen up the ears . . .
those are what shall has . . . with so much recording we can fix time
(illusion) . . . Coast Guard helicopter flies by (secretly) shouting . . . get
off now, now get off . . . so I move on (just a little). We eye-scavenge
the beach for anything of use or value . . . instead there is the color
of white sliding back to silver then gray, tan and sand . . . still sort
of time . . . (In all this change we pick out patterns . . . our rhythms
against its . . . multi-rhymed universe . . . systems within systems
interbumping each other in the aspects we chose and build our rhythms
to know . . .) the shells, rocks . . . funny image of a notebook, pen and
me walking by the sea to all the people who just came down to the
beach to get cool, or hot, relax or do something and nothing . . . driven
needs . . . Poochies eating seaweed . . . (flash of impending death!) . . .
a dead shark . . . (nature's way and away) . . . a new crab shell . . . (who

am I to think, "well, it put me here—now it can take me away." Well, it can and it does) . . . a big foot rock…(only not now, please not now . . . the only fear is in the Now . . . forever fixed now . . . is that death? While all else continues to change, you stay there, fast diminishing then, then, very then???? Is that death? "This is not dying" . . . Tomorrow Never Knows say the Beatles).

A brush of sea-grass — a cut off old giant broom . . . fish bones, Poochie chews on . . . the ants on the board on which I sit. (The total internal view is nothing but frightening confusion.) . . . another dead shark. The fog sludge of grey no color beach . . . summer for . . . let me send you a box of earth works today . . . almost into town . . . hungry, coming down. The people start to be here, I have been alone in my own head until now (froze at the sight of others . . . couldn't write . . . dwell in silence). Have a cigarette monstrosity and watch the young girls, the slide skill of the surfers and their waves (who knows them better?). Poochie rolling in the smell of dead fish . . . dog arpege. An old collector of shells . . . she is a rarity to this beach. A lot of people now on the beach, warm and in town. The sun is felt easier here, no wind with the reflecting shell of the steeper cliffs . . . a lobster claw and Poochie eating a shark's fin…

Turn off the beach, silence, downtown . . . pick a nasturtium, eat it (remembering e.e. cumming's directive "perhaps it is better to eat flowers and not be afraid") . . . tart cabbage taste . . . raw burning in the back of the mouth . . . take care of business . . . mail, pick it up . . . groceries, pick 'em up . . . eat another nasturtium . . . burn, baby, burn . . . surfers and young girls going to the beach . . . the old shell collector in her corvair-falcon-hotentot-american-made dreammobile taking off back to her city . . . jets low overhead sweeping the coast as they always do . . . writing on the fence in front of a drummer's house who believed in signs . . . past the usually empty tennis court in the little park for the little town . . . Youth goes by with its hands in its Hip pockets . . . raging furies in mad nowheres inside . . . another nasturtium and a little more focusing all the energies on this writing . . . white daisies in front yards faintly green fenced . . . perhaps this is 1890 . . . (by the electromagnetically shaved grass, cuticured sidewalk and steel flowers) . . . the heavy waxen leaves . . . a miniature cultured pansy only 3 inches high and two full blooms . . . groaning. A pear shaped dog, whistling boys and a softly strummed guitar behind the hedges, then it starts whistling and asks the time . . . 2:30 . . . people on the sidewalk path and in the street . . . roses . . . many flower smells . . . chirping of innumerable birds . . . close buzzing of insects . . . an occasional slow buzz of a single engine plane . . . yellow blooms, ivy, gates, pink roses and the smell of horses . . . dogs smelling each other into the street . . . the slowing of cars for the sacred act . . . a Porsche pulls away from the post office . . . expansion of time . . . neatly shaved hedge . . . many cars and into post office.

A letter from the welfare department . . . more, more, endless legal forms to fill out . . . the last of mint . . . hello of a young girl . . . I signed the damn letter and remailed it . . . bills . . . still got to walk around the corner and to the store. A young girl goes by in Dutch wooden shoes . . . my stepson is working in a yard with a friend making a dollar and a quarter an hour . . . five bicycles in a front yard . . . cars turning corners . . . roses . . . the corner presbyterian who was rocked . . . we could develop into fantasy once the juices get going . . . still the burn of nasturtium . . . a familiar cat . . . a big black dog with a scarred right eye smells Poochie . . . licks her ear as Poochie sits down . . . a car full of old Californians . . . two young pierced ears walk by silent and intimidated by my stopping to write . . . pass the only gas station and two triumphed college men ordering 3 dollars worth of america's blood sweet savage . . . across the street . . . "real" estate office combined with Christian Science . . . a gallery of old California . . . rusty spurs $3.00 . . . palm trees . . . one college gentleman looks at me from behind his mustached soul and buzzes off down the street . . . two girls, many panties ago . . . the swallows orange and blue diving in and out from under the roof of this community center where I stand to write for a second . . . (remembering the rock and tactical squad imported of law and order revenge . . . sweeping the empty street and sleeping beach . . . year ago fear, here) Clump, Clump of wooden shoes again.... the waving long black hair ties with a string just above the shoulders . . . bearded dealers and an old scarred painter . . . ladder and coveralls . . . young giggle of girls swinging a brown paper bag . . . music twice . . . overlapping voices . . . pianos . . . violins . . . the swallows . . . palms. Poochie sitting still beside me., looking out into the light quiet town from beneath this darkened shelter of a roof . . . blues being sung . . . two old men with pipes on an elevated porch across the street talking with folded arms . . . now, hands in their pockets, now gesturing, one hand out and pointing . . . a crow awkwardly walks down the driveway beside the restaurant, between bushes of roses, through the roof and into the air, cawing Smiley's, Snarley's, Scowley's . . . many songs . . . frying of meats and fish . . . summer business . . . wooden shoes again . . . the voice of a female racing driver "How much do you pay to drive what you want?" . . . clumping on a piano . . . cars starting up and pulling away from the store . . . sputtering trucks . . . vested long haired boys riding bicycles . . .

Now at the one and only owe-your-soul to the general store, standing in front, reading the bulletin board (our newspaper) and in to refuel . . . (motor patterns of thinking) . . . and Out. I sneak out of the way to get my commercial fix . . . break a pen trying to open the dried beef . . . tired when not writing or thinking it over . . . I open the potato chips . . . spill them all over the ground . . . hidden in the trees behind the greyhound bus stop . . . birds many rhythms twittering and chirping . . . the madness from which I just escaped . . . the STORE . . .

all those Want, Want, Wants, and there you are to Get, Get, Get...the many quiet shadings of green here and the clash red roar of 'In-The-Store' . . . consumed out . . . the ultimate junkie is the American consumer. Poochie has eaten all the spilled potato chips and it's time to hitch back up to the mesa . . . a cigarette and the super windowed space between me and where I am, so I can build word by word, where I am . . . the fleeting death image, now flees . . . I can buzz saw thru time not lagging as usual . . . the lower now on top . . . (illusion) . . . at least there is not the eternal premonition . . . many flies . . . the sun still not out . . . the Pepsi to be drunk . . . full stomach feeling . . . Poochie looking for more to eat . . . I feel too full . . . the throw away of that . . . I hitchhike home . . .

Get a ride with a very slow-moving couple (recounting this now at my desk . . . just home . . . with a copy of Charles Lamb's "Superannuated Man" lying open on the desk before me...) An older woman and VW young man driving slowly, she points out the wild-growing nasturtiums. I told them of taste . . . "You eat them" flabbergasted in his better-than-yours little tiny car, new by all means new . . . (I am still back there — the illusion comes easier now as the sun comes out on my paper . . . one foot on the never-got-to files . . . the other resting on Ruth's guitar case which is lain across a pile of little books of painters . . . a small pile of the world's art . . . the air filled with the counter tenor's duets of joy, signing "to celebrate the glories of the day" . . . sun through the open door . . . the time for the golden age to arrive . . . I become an instrument of music . . . 'Sing . . . Sing' . . .) slowly driving . . . "here and there," she says with a nasturtium in her hair, that she's afraid I might eat/// her voice is serene . . . I would paint her for that alone (Purcell's bass comes on against a chorus of sopranos . . . "Festival should be" . . . my head swims with the music and all its beatific "nos" . . . the sun again) . . . as they drop me off in front of the house with the little red door . . . "who does the painting?" and spun slowly off . . . out of their city existence to spend it here.

It took Charles Lamb "six and thirty years" to get loose . . . mine took six teaching years, many chemicals and much new thinking to uncondition the reflex. "Rejoicing" sings Purcell's celebration of his time, his place, of the very art itself . . . and a vast chorus explodes in total joy . . . the sun comes out in visible, tiny waves across this paper . . . the light softly fades . . . the music quietens . . . the birds sing madly . . . Ruth is with me now . . . it's a good life and continues to get better . . . having done more . . . She starts to say I spent too much money at the store. She says I show no restraint . . . "Touch, touch the lute and wake the heart" . . . Purcell still running through the head) No responsibility with money, all on the art . . . a little insane . . . sometimes more than others . . .

June 17, 1969

BOBBIE LOUISE HAWKINS

Rainbow

Over the lagoon   faint mist
soft air informs my skin
I breathe it in

                and see
                the colors shining there

A room far off in time and place
your face awash in color
your legs and all your body

                your face
                awash in color

your eyes adored me then
colors of air around me
a room of rainbows and bodies

                exhausted into
                only ecstasy

the air shimmered with it

                only ecstasy

bodies gone vast with it
a darling and hopeless geography
every touch rang for miles

Hopeless miles
away
and later

my windows filled with prisms
fill this room with rainbows
conjuring

                              a constellation
                              consolation

Over the lagoon as I go past
                              in sunlight

watching a gull's clean glide
breathing moist air
as if I breathed

                              your breath

Beyond the bird   a rainbow
your body arches across the sky
                              your body
fills the heaven
                              your eyes
                              are the sky
The soft air is your sigh

All Morning the Rain

is falling   all morning   long

In the clutter

unable

among the litter
of lives, the
shards, the broken bits
of first-life, second-
life, and the one after

and the next

Old photographs curl in the damp

We stay
caught, left over
with the litter that's left
to care for

Caught in life
Birth a debt
we keep paying

remembering

Depth and Heights
and Sweet Red Melons

in summertime
The bottom fell out of the market
over all the plains where melons
weren't worth the picking

Me and Donald-Gene walked the rows
lost in that field of bypassed crops

Kid's eye level on a clear day
in hot sun
Far as the eye can see melons
baking rips

Biggest watermelon patch
in all the wide world

Donald-Gene and me in overalls
got sick day after day walking
the rows eating watermelon hearts

Exacting and perfectionist
we did it this way:

      Pick a watermelon up
      to waist high and drop it
      When it's ripe it breaks

right open so the heart
sits high
on the seedy mess of the rest

One for him
One for me

I swear nobody ever
had it better

Own your body
as good a property
as any other.

Say, from this point
far as the eye can see,
It's me.

DUNCAN MC NAUGHTON

Tres

for Joanne Kyger

Kreatures of elaborate web spun betw. the bamboo
pole and honeysuckle vine, the endless wind, Tom's &
Angelica's roof, Joan's roof, eclectic unmoving houses snuggled where
the mesa slopes away, in the fore coyote bush is as tall as
Clark's eaves, Avenue of Roars

please, allow people all their strangeness & let the nightmare end
weirdness will not bring immortality though, that sad thought
of never-death for one, while others are swallowed by time

force of the breeze against silk, Kreatures sway on their sunlit
strands, but do not fall, enmeshed in white fairy, sticky flies

in Deutschland manufactured, of resin, mineral oil, etc., traps
the United States of America is the best place for the gradualisms
of social recreation, the free-est place
allowance, a place

to be, large and open for movement and inquisitiveness as
long as you have the money, my Hispanic-American brothers,
my English brethren, for when you wish (hic)
upon a star, makes no difference (burp) where you are

Mohowauuck

of beauty seen again and again in everything that happens
to us, til exhaustion lays spirit bare as we are,
hungover from reality and egotism like drunks
                              in the morning doing chores

closing doors, the night sky lights up in rose pink shocks of cloud
ermine, silent announcement of dawn courses overhead and drowns
gross me, the day grows colorful and definite like luck

and the autos go to and fro along the streets without my body
in the front seats of skill and certain provision for house and
homely application toward reward, possession, mutual care's neglect

but I wear it around my neck in the form
of the fourth, after turtle came the snake
after snake came the bird, after bird
we came, O the Mohawk girls laughed and laughed

I shook, I was hung 'cause they loved laughter
and made it slip around my neck and it turned to gold

Elegy

Oh, Peter Weston's dead

tall lean man not much
older than me

I think he said he came
from Pittsfield
always like a quiet man
especially if he is from Massachusetts
there seems to be so much
  to think about
he did three jobs for me: the garage
                    the front porch
                    in the back hall when we got the freezer
so, the lights're on.
He made the neatest bills I ever saw, printed, in pencil
every last thing, right to the penny

deep voice, long face, dark hair getting grey tied back, sad eyes

by his own hand, in his truck
                    what can be said
that the end hath come
I wish it hadn't quite so soon

for him.   don't say much to nothing
that was a man, wore suspenders and walked slow
who do you see about the ones we *lose*?

You don't, brother, you go downtown for some vodka
                                                        and look around the bar
someone's missing every time
until every one is gone

we were never here when we left
we never even came

They can take his card out from under the glass on the counter
in the hardware store
  means nothing

you keep, like Israel Potter, going home, but there's nothing left, some rocks
    and new trees where fences alone keep none out
 walk along a ridge hidden from the sun nowadays
that was clear meadow and farms. Whatever
made Peter happy sure didn't come his way much

the cloud passed over and you can't count the stars, there's too many
but you won't see that cloud again either, you won't see anything

again. However, I know I liked this man
and it's time to go back to Smiley's,
                                            quiet, "This town
                                                is dead"
                                            woman says
"I've been loving you too long" Otis Redding jukebox
you could say that about the world

that every night goes to sleep

I like a man, I like his arms
    I like a man when he gets older, I like the shape and
      what it feels like a man has to be
now that he is older and his body aches here and there, here
in the dark when the vodka goes down in the empty town
til your throat won't take it, it's time to go

Instinctively, Kirsten, amid the tedious noise of drunks
ruminatively, chuckling to herself, gets up
and comes over with a greyish single-paper joint.
For a drink she will have half of a tequila &
grapefruit juice
which costs fifty cents and I, another vodka.
After that, no words are exchanged. Pool is watched, the evening is over.

It's windy, raw outside.

ARAM SAROYAN

Love

The beauty of a summer evening . . .
The television on in the living room: The Waltons.
A book I like out there too.
But I sneak away to catch the day fading
Into the first minutes of the night.

To be a survivor of all this richness
And to live on, cherishing life, for its own sake.
Singing praises to its light and its night,
The pungency of color in a child's face,
The birth of ideas in the mind.

Outside the fog closes the scene in—
Pale mists the trees move behind.
Closer, the daisy bush just outside this window
Is immobile—the crowd of flowers
Stopped in windless color.

Empty, empty, as I am now—
As I always feared before but now merely notice.
I am time, not space; time to engage
In conversation, gentle interaction, with space.
To make love with the sure touch of time's favor.

No rush, no necessity to be finished—
An understanding with the world of pleasure
That is time itself—the pressure of a hand
Just so, no more the man than the woman,
And no more one another than love.

For Tom Clark

Big city boys come out
to the country, toy with

the idea
of becoming farmers, forgetting

their nervous systems for a while,
it almost seems easy (why

write poetry about dock strikes?)—
their wives cooperate with

nature so well, or seem to know
their own rhythm better

than men, creatures of crude habit
perhaps, an Orange Julius might hit

the spot
right now—they think, circling and

circling the precise matter of their own
home, and children come into this

as quickly as they find themselves
a place in it, meanwhile the planet spins

and keeps time perfectly with the Universe
like a guitar solo by Eric

Clapton (Derek & The Dominoes) it all
seems to fit, nothing impressionably wrong

or jarringly accurate, even—that too
becoming useless as we go on in this life,

soon to hit thirty, soon to hit twenty-nine,
and getting better all the time.

Day and Night

Like a drop
of ink
as it hits

the water—
the whole
glass

going black:
in death
and vision,

decompression—
the soul
united

across
space and
time;

the heart
that was
blind,

a healed thing,
whole.
This

is what
the poet knows
and how he

grows apart.
Oh foolish one,
oblivious

of broken
light:
the one contained

holds the day,
the one apart
the night

JIM BRODEY

Zither Dawn Ooze

Zither dawn ooze dripping from green rainbow tunnels
In vast cold upper canyon rills of Big Sur, cold
Lush vacant completely-filled with bear track & deer shit mound,
The music of frosted air particles BLAMELESSLY FALLEN past huts
That loom tiny as insect in overgrown sparse for heights.

Bell-tunes echo down the long canyon, fog propellants soothe out
Circling hawk dancers afloat on hazy green oxygen seas, looped
At dawn with some hikers near natural brush shrine, a beer can
Floating in this world's crystal cold lake dawn on petals of light.
In canyon-wall crink, snowy blue vapor pours from the rock-floor,
Upwards through heavy pant-legs, astounding everybody.

In those valleys, in these creeks of hollow daylight trash, in
My sleepingbag on the roof of the air, the wild zither sings
In my head. The body moves out of this whispering old green heart,
Taking me up into breezy glorious sensation jewel Heaven
Numb from the fevers of the words, and the quiet powers of the climb.

Words to the Music of the Future
for Tandy

wonderful balmy days happy as the daze is long & the quick
visions are rare and perfect

sand is blowing in the window but you'd probably call it soot

boogie sneeze bounces off the moon (Aries in Gemini)
wandering low & lovely skin-deep & plenty high
listening to birdees in the skull sing "Rip It Up"

dancing barefoot through powdery extract of Words
through hamburger planets
through a bright midnight

Brodey-voice published fragrant Peru lion tongue in a tone-deaf
temple trance on silver sliver of half-
radiant golden "whew!"

　Aether liber-
　　　ation

　sucks on spun
　　　　driven webs

to the cartoon universe : : : : Whitman's pictureless
　　　　　　　　　　　　　　　melodies

: : : : Ginsberg's absolute
body-truth

happy as the day be long
and wonderful

high on you

This Magic Moment

This magic moment
When the blue of the night
meets the gold of the day

Is sponsored in the future
by premonitions
of an America that is still magic America
Blue skies & clouds scrubbing
precipice wild berries and flying oats
marinated in big midair flurry
of stones

Yellow aspens
uncomputable parents of songs that beckon
Feel them stirring warmly within
and say nothing

Ballid

for Allan Ruppersberg

When the twilight is gone
And twilight comes into my head

That's when all thy trees are made more abundant
And water flows beneath gnarled roots of the heart

Of finest paisley earth chin
Bathing monsoon turbulence for any janitor of voyages

And a sea of tunes harvests the mourning land

And twilight basks in badland's silent buttes
Thy vaportrails signal propulsion to Joshua quiet

And gone have been our trees
And my heart rises appreciative through late Spring rains

Water to the suffocating land & breath to me
Cools the mountainside herds with glorious music

And turbulence ceases to exist

And man finds in oxygen what he but thought he had found in
twilight

Tunes flow through water as twice familiar is the fish to air
Whose lips catch all available light off the bathing land

And buttes radiate that sterner stuff stuck in our heads
And breath clogs mucous passages to my heart

Music deploys the hand-held turbulence
Continuous voyages dawning in puffs of quiet cloud

DIANE DI PRIMA

April Fool Birthday Poem for Grandpa

Today is your
birthday and I have tried
writing these things before,
but now
in the gathering madness, I want to
thank you
for telling me what to expect
for pulling
no punches, back there in that scrubbed Bronx parlor
thank you
for honestly weeping in time to
innumerable heartbreaking
italian operas for
pulling my hair when I
pulled the leaves off the trees so I'd
know how it feels, we are
involved in it now, revolution, up to our
knees and the tide is rising, I embrace
strangers on the street, filled with their love and
mine, the love you told us had to come or we
die, told them all in that Bronx park, me listening in
spring Bronx dusk, breathing stars, so glorious
to me your white hair, your height your fierce

blue eyes, rare among italians, I stood
a ways off looking up at you, my grandpa
people listened to, I stand
a ways off listening as I pour out soup
young men with light in their faces
at my table, talking love, talking revolution
which is love, spelled backwards, how
you would love us all, would thunder your anarchist wisdom
at us, would thunder Dante, and Giordano Bruno, orderly men
bent to your ends, well I want you to know
we do it for you, and your ilk, for Carlo Tresca,
for Sacco and Vanzetti, without knowing
it, or thinking about it, as we do it for Aubrey Beardsley
Oscar Wilde (all street lights
shall be purple), do it
for Trotsky and Shelley and big/dumb
Kropotkin
Eisenstein's Strike people, Jean Cocteau's ennui, we do it for
the stars over the Bronx
that they may look on earth
and not be ashamed.

Revolutionary Letter #4

Left to themselves people
grow their hair.
Left to themselves they
take off their shoes.
Left to themselves they make love
sleep easily
share blankets, dope & children
they are not lazy or afraid
they plant seeds, they smile, they
speak to one another. The word
coming into its own: touch of love
on the brain. the ear.

We return with the sea, the tides
we return as often as leaves, as numerous
as grass, gentle, insistent, we remember
the way,
our babies toddle barefoot thru the cities of the universe.

Revolutionary Letter #9

advocating
the overthrow of government is a crime
overthrowing it is something else
altogether. it is sometimes called
revolution
but don't kid yourself: government
is not where it's at: it's only
a good place to start:
    1. kill head of Dow Chemical
    2. destroy plant
    3. MAKE IT UNPROFITABLE FOR THEM
to build again.
i.e., destroy the concept of money
as we know it, get rid of interest,
savings, inheritance
(Pound's money, as dated coupons that come in the mail
to everyone, and are void in 30 days
is still a good idea)
or, let's start with no money at all and invent it
    if we need it
or, mimeograph it and everyone
    print as much as they want
    and see what happens

declare a moratorium on debt
the Continental Congress did
'on all debts public and private'
& no one 'owns' the land

it can be held
for use, no man holding more
than he can work, himself and family working

let no one work for another
except for love, and what you make above your needs be given to the
tribe
a Common-Wealth

None of us knows the answers, think about
these things.
The day will come when we have to know
the answers.

Revolutionary Letter #13

now let me tell you
what is a Brahmasastra
Brahmasastra, hindu weapon of war
near as I can make out
a flying wedge of mind energy
hurled at the foe by god or hero
or many heroes
hurled at a problem or enemy
cracking it

Brahmasastra can be made
by any or all
can be made by all of us
straight or tripping, thinking together
like: all of us stop the war
at nine o'clock tomorrow, each take one soldier
see him clearly, love him, take the gun
out of his hand, lead him to a quiet spot
sit him down, sit with him as he takes a joint
of viet cong grass from his pocket . . .

Brahmasastra can be made
by all of us, tripping together
winter solstice
at home, or in park, or wandering
sitting with friends
blinds closed, or on porch, no be-in
no need

to gather publicity
just gather spirit, see the forest growing
put back the big trees
put back the buffalo
the grasslands of the Midwest with their herds
        of elk and deer
put fish in clean Great Lakes
desire that all surface water on the planet
be clean again. Kneel down and drink
from whatever brook or lake you conjure up.

Revolutionary Letter #14

are you prepared
to hide someone in your home indefinitely
say, two to six weeks, you going out
for food, etc., so he never
hits the street, to keep your friends away
coolly, so they ask no questions, to nurse
him, or her, as necessary, to know
'first aid' and healing (not to freak out
at the sight of torn or half-cooked flesh)
to pass him on at the right time to the next
station, to cross the canadian border, with a child
so that the three of you
look like one family, no questions asked
or fewer, to stash letters, guns, or bombs
forget about them
till they are called for, to KEEP YOUR MOUTH SHUT
not to 'trust'
even your truelove, that is,
lay no more knowledge on him that he needs
to do his part of it, a kindness
we all must extend to each other in this game

ROBERT CREELEY

Rain

Things one sees through
a blurred sheet of glass,
that figures, predestined,
conditions of thought.

•

Things seen through
plastic, rain sheets,
trees blowing in a blurred
steady sheet of vision.

•

Raining, trees blow,
limbs flutter, leaves
wet with the insistent
rain, all over, everywhere.

•

Harry will write
Mabel on Monday.
The communication
of human desires

flows in an apparently
clear pattern, aftersight,
now they know
for sure what it was.

If it rains, the woods
will not be so dry
and danger averted,
sleep invited.

Rain (2)

Thoughtful of you, I was
anticipating change in
the usual manner. If the rain

made the day the unexpected,
in it I took a place.
But the edge of the room

now blurred, or the window
did, or you, sitting, had
nonetheless moved away.

Why is it an empty house
one moves through, shouting
these names of people there?

Bolinas and Me . . .

for Stan Persky

Bolinas and me.
Believe me.

Roy Kiyooka
not here

says that.
Say this.

The human,
the yearning,

human situation
wanting something to be,

which is.
What's wanted?

Let the man put the gas in
your car, John, e.g.,

complete doing what
you wanted him to.

Have *done* with it?
Ham on rye.

The sea, the drive
along the coast in L.A.

I remember Joanne. I
want to. She's

lovely, one says.
So she is. So

are you too.
Or one. Have

done with it.
You see that

line of rocks out there?
Water, waves, two

dead sea lions,
says Peter. He's

lovely. All of them.
Let's walk down

to the beach, see
the sea, say.

If you love someone,
you'd better believe it,

and/or you could,
could write

that all night,
all right. All wrong.

All—isn't enough.
I want to get going. Here's love.

Drive home, up through the mountains,
dense fog. See the car lights

make way of it. See
the night, all around.

Bleed, into the toilet,
two nights, two days,

away from whatever,
go home, and stay there?

I want to walk around here,
look at the people, pretty,

look at the houses, stop in
the bar, get the mail, get

going again, somewhere.
One, two, three, four.

Husbands and fathers.
Sweet love, sweet love.

The kids come
by on bicycles, the little,

increasingly large
people, in the rain.

The liquor store lights
shine out in the night,

and one is walking, going,
coming, in the night.

Holy place we stand in,
these changes—Thanksgiving,

in the circle of oaks,
the sun going west, a glowing

white yellow through the woods.
To the west all the distance.

Things move. You've come to here
by one thing after another, and are here.

Flat thoughts in recalling
something after. Nostalgic twist

of everything so thought—a
period of thought here.

Hair falling, black tangle,
standing in front of the fire,

love dancing, silent, a figure,
a feeling, felt and moving here.

After all it speaks
less is saying more. It, it—

the hunk of wood is
not burning.

Marriage burns, soars—
all day the roar of it

from the lovely barnspace.
The people, the plenitude of all

in the open clearing, sun-
light, lovely densities. I am

slowly going, coming home. *Let
go, let go of it.* Walking

and walking, dream of those
voices, people again, not

quite audible though I can
see them, colors, forms,

a chatter just back on the ear,
moving toward them, the edge

of the woods. Again and
again and again, how

insistent, this blood one
thinks of as in

the body, these hands,
this face. Bolinas sits on the ground

by the sea, sky
overhead.

JOEL WEISHAUS

Eucalyptus

"Down south to tall forests (Kari-Jarrah-
all Eucalyptus) of Pemberton . . . "

That's Australia. To California
they brought the wrong species
for hardwood harvests,

though Blue Gum's good
for sucking-up fog.

PHILIP WHALEN

Bill Brown

"Nobody likes automobiles
Unless they are trying to kick
A habit like Jean Cocteau."

The War

A handsome young Vietnamese guy from Burlington, Vermont
Just now got it right in the neck

15:X:67

October Food

Pine-tree child soaks in a teapot
Chrysanthemum perfume soup and a
Seasnail boiling in his shell, that I
May live forever

International Date Line, Monday / Monday 27:XI:67

Here it comes again, imagination of myself
Someplace in Oregon woods I sit on short
Wide unpainted wooden cabin steps
Bare feet wiggle toes in dirt and moss and duff
The sun shines on me, I'm thinking about all of us
How we have and haven't survived but curiously famous
Alive or dead—X has become a great man, Y very nearly
Greater, perhaps in some other dimension, Z apparently
Still in a frenzy pursuit of universal admiration, fame & love

And there's LeRoi seated in TIME magazine wheelchair
Head bashed in under hospital bandage
Blood all running down the side of his face

Capitalistic Society Destroyed by the Contradictions within Itself. (Second Five-Year Plan.)

feeble claw blanket grab disappear foot hog
crackling Oklahoma dustbowl (Virgil Thompson)
whisker tickles shoulder. eye sinus bulge
with ½ & ½ cock numb and warm, all body skin slack
and thrown into soft folds except stony heels
death's crumby elbow no breath asthma drag all
joints arthritic ankylose threat night sound
terror as of ages 1 through now I cannot accept
the ending of a day no more light I cannot wait
for night when bed fucking blowing jacking-off is
possible at least naked safe pleasure

5:VII:68

Duerden's Garage, Stinson Beach

1

Honeybee struggles in gardenspider web
Hook feet crochet a silky tomb
Will it work itself to death before the spider eats it?
Sunshines through its back: black and amber tank

as long as that
                    the bluejay flies
                        hollers
            B L E A K

TYRANNICAL ARACHNID, HENCE!

That's that. Lie down . . . .

                                    amber tank? Look again.

            G O N E
Holes in the web, several strands roped together by the
                    spinning of that bee body
                    polygonal vacancies
                                    GONE
(far too little time for the spider to have wrapped it away
to the cypress tree, to the edge of the roof, down
                    to the Chinese whoopee bush)

Flew the coop. I wouldn't help or hinder.
Hungry victory!

2

O Duerden! Enormous profundities thrust themselves
Amongst our sensoria which ignore them;
Profound immensities engulf the visible present dispensation!
Torment! Freak! Savage tremble illiterate musculature
True human speech of Maya glyph: BAKTUNS. KATUNS.
Accurately stoned American time before the frauds of pro-
        fessional history's shameful rage!

Sweat, voluminous agey brain! Draw nearer and
Melt down in Poesy's ravening violet flames

Honey song perfume! Look where my periwig smoulders!
California sherry feeds the fire with amber potable:
Sweet flowing sunbeams trapped in crystal,

            (H I A T U S)

Waste emotion. Entire mountains removed, the gravel sifted in order
to locate a nickel's worth of gold: In such manner the hours of my life
here sift away. Ashes of burnt paper, desiccation of the spirit, imbecility
of mind, withering of the heart which signalize my decline into
ignominious death & obscure grave.
        VERSUS MEI HABEBUNT ALIQUANTUM NOCTIS . . .
        to top it all off, Duerden's cat, Alfy, has decided to fall
desperately in love with me 9:30 at night when he ought to be at home
23:X:68 Received notice that I must find somewhere else to live before
the first part of 1969. I wonder where. 31:X Pioneer violets bloom today.

ANNE WALDMAN

Jolt

Man grappling with wasp,
Bolinas summer 1968
is not the same man grappling
with the same wasp,
Bolinas summer 1971

Same man, different wasp

Beware the different wasp
her bite

Bite sandwich with gusto
put swim suit on
re-enter

water
in being in with you

All "equally talented hotshots"
stand out from the crowd

All equally talented
lettuce and tomato
sandwiches
with cloud

Equally talented Jim Morrison
dead in bath

riders on the storm
riders on the storm
            into this world we're thrown

a temperature jolt

dead

death

be still, being very still

July 3, 1971

Spin Off

for Lewis, Phoebe & Ocean MacAdams

Throw dice

Horse Latitudes

I want to go to the bar

I need sleep

Somewhere between Spain and the Old World
is Spain

Somewhere between Spain and the New World
is
        calm   cloudless   sky

Horses' bones asleep in the deep

Did I hear "noise"?

Insolent racoon

Outlaw inside LAW

"I'm not *out*, mean of course I make mistakes"

Town

Now
won

Tom over

Bow down
& incorporate this earth

Walk free in I'll call it MacAdams lagoon,

        gulls

man
Phoebe
child
deer
bird
dog
simple or
loud
lassitude

flutter of wings

Or no sound at all

Or night fall, and one by one the stars . . .

Haze you out tonally

Fog does the rest

"No such thing as dirty work in this town!"

Two minutes of silence, please
For the 4 Founders of Ornithology

"I'm serious, these coasts . . ."

Sober
Management

(pause)

"Does a ring around the moon mean rain?"

If so: rain

Get crackin' on the shingles
Sweetie pie
You wanna keep your lady dry?

Ouch is my hammer

rung
on
evol
ut
ion
ary
lad
der

  (note: West Coast uses "my old lady")

Let's see
gaggle of geese on a sky full of flamingoes
shattering our stillness
of morning?

wake me up my
totem poem
motets
om tete: *Places to Go*

Brain circulation: 100%

Thinking: zero

Wind: eucalyptus

&
tip top, Don Allen

Find myself waking

8:30 am
September
Bolinas
Seventy-one

As a scrambled hen

squawk, yawk

"Anne, that's not how you address the chickens!
All scrambled -- hush!"

(an authoritative Philip Whalen)

10 tiny messages
from the flame people

1. listen to the whistle   fog
2. run along
3. but I do I do

4: arrow, dart, tree, burn

5. paw
6. print
7. gypsy
8. long

9. sweetened
10. in memory

anathema
of an eye gaze
useless blood shed
behind prison wall

No no no
Again again again

Zip/Viet Nam

Ready, ear
Ready, Ocean

Near
You
Nearer you
Being child

"How get so overcrowded?"

Wonderful babies of enlightened beings
coo in ear

Zip zip zip a walking tableaux
of agates

"eye of gods"

A bevy of quail shoot
up into tree

Car come
& when car come

a bevy of quail
 shoot
        up
    into
            tree
when   car   come
car come

Joanne: there are no limits

to people as people

Feelings are true

The space is ours now

Men behind bars now
But why?

Axis to grind

You came out
spinning
skulking from the library

Come in, attractive as poetry
Now begin

PHOEBE MACADAMS

Things

He pushed the car over the embankment and watched the lady fix it.
"The lady knows," he said, drinking his coffee in the warm air. The
fish swam in their water which is clean now that I don't feed them
so much. Willie looks at the black-handled scissors and I wave at the
flowers. "Everybody in this town is somebody they're not supposed to
be," he says. And I? I look forward to walking in the cool breezy sun.
Stars.

Storms

When the storms raged across Europe, I went upstairs with a cup of hot chocolate. We said no to global war, but I got used to the picture of you dragging yourself on your elbows towards a gun and both of you lying dead under the rubble.

Now you come and wrap yourself around me. You sit next to me on the ground and lean your head on the bench. I caress your cheek and hair and kiss the edges of your mouth as if you were actual. Sometimes I go to sleep like this and when I wake you are gone and I don't miss you. But sometimes we have loved everywhere and then I am always longing. Before your arms had strength and your hand allowed us. Now it won't, so I hurry home behind my children and nag them to button up their capes. Sometimes I steal away with you and hold you in the shadows. I have learned to do this, but then I must stop as we edit out our errors and return to our lives. You may visit. We are here, where we always are.

One

I look down at my hand and wonder:
Is that nail really a part of me?
Then I remember:
Sweet touch and kisses.
Oh, then it was all part of me.

Bolinas Journal

Third day of rain. More storms coming in. Peas staked. Weeds pulled around the spinach and lettuce. The losses come in with the storms and bleak weather. We keep going, hermetically sealed with a book somewhere.

A large portion of the town collapses with the flu. Is our health a dead man? They ride across the gap on a well-trained dart and return with health. This is a fair trade, but O God, have I fallen in love with a shadow? I slip away with a living shade and fade out of difficulty. Will I disappear completely? The ruinous weather continues. I stay inside and restore myself with a holiday so I can offer you a cup of tea. There are battles raging about town. Someone brushes up against me, dressed in full battle regalia. I say I prefer tea and hot chocolate. Also, I remember when yes meant no and no meant yes. It was confusing then, too. Now, I look at the treetops swaying in the appreciative breeze.

Icicle

He's a body guard with a dozen red roses. The nature of icicles, voices.
We were speaking of the nature of icicles over a dozen red roses. The
water is dripping. The fall is over. The body guard is out of town.
Icicles are forming. Much depends upon what has gone before. The
breeze at Gold Hill. A sock on the table. A handful of red roses. A
lover circulates in black lace. He presses his hips against me. He hands
me a rose. In California the ravager smiles. The telephone explodes.
I did not want to be so moved! I did not mean to be so moved! O yes
I did. Pausing at the top of an icicle, it slides on what has gone before
and freezes in the air. I am speaking of the nature of icicles, a handful
of red roses: so steadfast! so sweet! I am thinking loosely of alone. The
stream was fed by a high glacier. The sun shines, and then, I am not an
icicle! Sliding down the tongue, the back, the mountain, the breath.
Sliding through the phone. Five to two. I have always loved tongues,
ears and red roses.

Wall of Words

on the occasion of a reading by John Ashbery

I was listening to a line of words. I had opened all the doors and
windows and the words were coming through becoming walls, floor,
ceiling and chair I was sitting on. I lay down and rolled over and drifted
off and came back, sat up, listening. I was thinking about New York, put
my feet up, and still the words were coming. Again I opened, listening.
Later at the party I was still listening. We had been talking earlier in the
car about how hard it is to be naked in front of strangers. I was wearing
a long purple print dress with a low neckline. Bobbie commented it
would be an easy party to leave which made us feel better. Then I was
talking to Gerard. He didn't remember coming into our house dressed
in white and meditating on the rug. I hadn't believed that act, anyway,
and he had given up T.M. The curl in his lip was back and he was tough
and naughty and ambitious again. Thank heavens. He said he would
give me five years to get my act together. He went to get a strawberry
for my wine. Then we were talking about firewood in Bolinas, and
thieves. John said he didn't like the feeling of hot lips. He said he was
afraid of getting burnt. He smiled a hideous smile and walked away, the
line of words inside him. Michael put his hand on my stomach. I looked
for a while into his tender eyes. Then he and Bobbie were talking in
an articulate fashion about everything that had just happened. She was
wearing a brown dress and sweater, brown hose and her fur coat. Joanne
was wearing a bluish dress, sandals, many elegant shawls, two exquisite
rings of ruby, pearl and diamond. We had bought our dresses at the
same store. Then I stopped listening and we were running down the
stairs, laughing. Michael said he was a French restaurant. We got in the
car and ate burritos over the hill to Bolinas. Bobbie drove. Bobbie and
Joanne were talking, I was looking out at the stars, listening.

EBBE BORREGAARD

6 Songs
Sung with Autoharp accomp. 1970

I ALWAYS WILL BE HIDDEN from you
you may think it's perfection
        but it's really protection

I wld tell you the true story
        if you'd trust my poor glory.

<< >>

MY BOLINAS

I am all that aspirations will contend
you, young of the east westward wending
It is for you I have been loved over and over
In alien temples, in homefields, where I was a rover

We have waited since the first celestial dawn
yr loveliness to meet, the power of our Loving
as the principle law this univers abides
We lukt in its size & within us it is hiding

And I have waited out all my unthinking days
for yr glad light inbreathing, inothering my ways
As I tript on roots of misery & ate leaves of despair
looting the Stars for yr incandescent hair

See all the continuum knows the Cosmic Folly
which wld allow the human Ebbe no Angelic Dolly.

<< >>

WHEN I WAS YOUNGER than a
fourleaft green clover
I danced well before Atmos
in the Kingdom of Trarys

& I watched my wee figure
sliding and striding
to the tunes of a Rover
who was my Kingling

He'd sit me down
so patient & wearing
whispering storys when I was
tired of earthly glorys

I think his heart my body
surely stops beating
when my pale human form
glows like a throne of old

Being far from the barricades
of everyday living
for I flew up and downsteps
& floated over seawide puddles

I never trusted those hairy
old people who showd you things
it didn't matter how
or why you did them ever

And sung in the chair
of our gleaming white body
the Oldman and I
wld fly off asinging

We'd laugh our fool heads off
at the dreams of other dreamors
bouncing like bubbles
encircling the earth

One night I did see
a vast and boiling ocean
of all the colors
in the rainbow I guess

it was our Sun
& thru it we were going.
Deep in the center
we past a Hermit praying

Tho what he sayd
I barely remember, its like
In the Ebyss of light
I am drowndead

Save me O Lord
the paths I have walkt
are now running rivers
But a short sword

I have, defending my Dragons
—And we've seen all
that wants to be seen
And we've seen all that wants
to be seen

<< >>

I PROSPECT IN THE COLD
courageous, chill & bold
yet I respect an old master
beside Jack, its Mister Blake
& Kate : bookmakers most great.
When verbatim, them I make
As best I can, lament for the
taker, the measurer, the fakir
and forsaker.

I warm up very fast
you can feel my blazing blast
and you can see me going faster
Here on like icing on an angel
baby's cake. And there it is to take
Flashers on but ready just wait
Before us fragrant gardens with
gentle rushing streams and all
yr ageless dreams.

Excuse me while I rinse
Now, don't I look the prince
In the confusion of rain wind & wave
I hear the shore the tides obey
What, as I repair to sleep anticipating
the stillness of the inner sea, the
feeble distances, a moonruled existence
that down there—what on our shores
have we to share.

<< >>

I AM A BRIDGE over the sea of
life. O I am a pig for Love, I
need no sure vessel as I swim
thruout existence, spread out
yr arms, give me no alms, I
bestow on you, I have nothing
to keep—but it gives my eye
no pleasure to see extasy asleep
in so great aplace, out of my wits
—wake up—love the makers of your face.

It's so easy first you breathe out,
then you breathe in, that's
all there is to it, I am the
goal, I am all others, death
is a gay young girl who pre-
cedes me. The feast is perpet-
ually in progress, yet she pre-
tends to hear footsteps follow-
ing, in the moonless night of
her mind.

Come, We do Not so Fly on
the ground, thru memory, in
the sky—nor anywhere, but
that when we fly, we are
faithfully flying, as
everyplace is everywhere, ex-
clude nothing from the 'race,'
even as you tell me what has
been troubling you, the spear
of yr Reason wounds the body
thru. What endures changes,
everything will pass away and
who will hear what you will say.

And You Think Wisdom what has not
been done and the fine line
of negation—just as you define
desire and love thinking them
the dove and the crow—what you
will have dies without a summer
season.

when the late four billion years
died to give you one
even showing you the gate

                    to one.

<< >>

WHAT TO ME THE WIND of revolution
which vanity wld fill my sail
so for here the trouble upon the ocean
the cottage bracing against the storm
my ship takes it passage
as the rain courses upon the tiles of the roof
and when in the cool cool shade of summer
when all the world is at peace
I will call to you from the cunning waters
singing far more substantial than the earth
beneath the weight of your feet
and I will sob for you bitterly
how great my ship
never near you except when under the moon

JOANNE KYGER

A Testimony for Ebbe and Angela on their Wedding, November 29, 1970

Way up in the sky is a shimmering silver figure
She's a tall lady in white
Small leaves are wound in her hair

                                   she's up there all right
        and she's down here too
        in a pool at night, bathed by her own

  silver light

                dear stuff

              is the union of sides

            & that is the identity
            out of this self to you
            this self to you

                  that breaks into green wood clearing
                    a song succinct & cheerful, open and generous

                    •

We'd forgotten if it wasn't
still around
    that profecy
into which I can step to fill
myself •not• I
    is only life
and what you do with it.

            The sky people go to heaven
            up the sky pole
            and they came back
            and tell what they have found—

                and the far shore, low dunes
            with water against them
            long low
                long dunes
                sand banks
                    foliage dotting
                the coast & curves
            into the golden harbor—
                    thru the narrow harbor
                mouth opening
                it's a beautiful golden harbor
            & trees too on the shore of the
            harbor, the boats
        are somewhat oriental
    one millennium & a half old.

Walking further into that land there very low,
    rolling hills gently rising & falling

and the brush moves into trees
    moving up on the low slopes
and the brush moves up into the trees
   and into a grove & into a center
   in the clearing, birds hop
     shyly on the trees
     & a big white owl flaps
  his tracy wings & a hawk
    gets chased by the crows &
   the monarch butterflys & the
     gold finch.
              And Ebbe and Angela
have no clothes on but they're
nice and brown from the sun; and
they go around playing with the
animals, the giraffes & the
tortoise & pick hibiscus from the trees
and small sweet smelling orchids
too and some delicious oranges. And
then they lay down on a beautiful
bed of moss with ferns all
around. And then Ebbe falls asleep
& he doesn't notice Angela
for a while & when he wakes
up she says, here's a nice red
apple for you to eat deer.

        And let's Go!
      Wow! they're off
         She's a good cook.

It's all returning.

             because it sounds so good to them
                 it brings them all together
             because they are all together
                    they grow
                 because they grow
                    they are strong
             because they are strong
                 they sound good
             because they sound good
                 everyone wants to hear it
             because everyone wants to hear it
                 it brings them all together.

                    FATHER TIME
                 & MOTHER EARTH

who lived with the beasts and the free growing animals.
one
two
what pours into you

she approaches the edge

sometimes when I am neither happy nor unhappy
whenever sea I go to green meadow under eucalyptus tree
                    and black cows
             beller from the other side of the power towers
                        probably where the little huts are on the beach
     and fly down the hill & under the barbed wire where the dogs go

snif snif the easy way
like the rabbits too
and he emerged safely out her womb
and put his head back up again
but sliding down was the only way he got born
&
the whole everything a life was shimmering

Well even if these things are called animal
even tho I ride on top of a great pig
even tho you go walking down the street to think about it
even tho the ocean and the mountains
even tho the laurel too is wound tight in the locklets
even tho I look up to you and you look up to me
even tho we are flat plains
even tho I'm a river bottom
even tho the sun comes up in me
even tho my roots are found and flow flow
are as far past as the great deep stretch of space back
is carried in me as your mother
and I come forth
wild life
shaking
like when sun hits the water
like when under star fish sea
like when he or she arrives
riding the elephant
even tho I won't walk the streets tonight
even tho you are an ocean boundless and bottomless
because I am your power and his too
I won't go away from your ever returning and coming back

of course it must be a strong rider

lavish

you two

lay down

upon a bed of lace

making this!

bend softly like wheat

across a summer day and the black snow

And Angela will make some soup

for the both of you and

some French bread

with butter plus

a couple, no many more than that of

celery, carrots,

a bowl of nuts

that good strawberry colored

tea!

turn on! the sun

speckles   down thru

pagions of per sion writing

I thought about you last night, and a great blue heron came up
on to the porch so I could see him thru my window. And I met him
again on the beach, and all the animals came close
and spoke to me, and I balanced this all night long
for everyone they spoke to me

all gods in the human breast

I know

true friendship

AH! MEN!

First There Were Giants

First there were giants
and then getting consciousness
    I mean mind
 aware, became
        gods
  & then man
 came out of gods
as it was more
      familiar
& then
  god was above
   them & then
  god became
  man again
     &
 now
not man anymore not
  god anymore
one mind
        to leave
  one mind holds on
I mean the body
  walks with feet
on the earth
     the head out
  into the stars

I'm not just one
   all past & present
      here
      face down
               by pacific
  reaches who who
     as it is grounded the new
spirit brought down *here*
by the mother helped
 by the father
   who throws his waste
      spirit away
 no no aids
  & becomes spirit
   no body is left
  as his support
 in the sky in substance
or coming around again
  into new bodies never
   lets go of an
       intensity taking
it on into
     Angels
   in you
   on you
   with you

Under the Green Light

Under the green light
you see when the new spirit comes along
  it had to get on top
 of the old spirits
so the old spirits
  were pushed underground
 by the wait
   & they're only dark
 when seen from the perspective
 of light because the new spirit
  saw them as raw
 untidy, out of order
and they only moved at night
 and tried to be out of sight
 forgotten in this dusty corner
   oh   eeek get that spider
 out of here
   and under the ground in seed holes
   and hanging from trees upside down
   and lost souls
  who don't know which
   way to go, dark or light
    good or bad
      say oh leader of the lost
     promise me the company
  of the dark oh the passing
   smell the shimmer of evil oh

it grows like a snake
moves like the strongest
most beautiful dream in the world

green flashes
sparks
cups

TOM CLARK

Inside the Dome of the Taj Mahal

Chant's Operations

I chant
you chant
he, she or it chance

•

The trees and seas
Were as they are
When I was here before.

A strange unease
Made those of these
As they were where they are.

•

Moonrise expresses spaces
in air, tides in the sea

illustrate old stresses
in nasal reef-voice, ah harmony
shimmering beyond choice
The silver surfer stands there, streaming

long hair laid out
across the night so transposed.

•

Bad Vibes Ahead

Tough City

•

Barbecue Bob's impersonal space
is mine to dispose—

hyaline aeroliths in ether.

•

condition conditions,
conditions condition.

"The condition my condition is in"

•

Slomo replays of pro linebackers bumping into backs (Dick Butkis)

•

Genetic Requistion Form

He's got to be straight
We don't want a bent one

•

6 a.m.

I die inside Kathy's Clown.
I don't know who I am.

•

That mind should exist inside meat's an insane fact.

•

No More Rehearsals!

•

Those good round radio tones
Some of the most peaceful sounds I know

•

If you just want to drift off and disappear
then these are the ones
                    to do it with:

The Songs of the Hump-Backed Whale
Tintinabulations
Inside the Dome of the Taj Mahal

The Book of Love

for Joanne Kyger

There is a new arrogance in the dip of her back and the proud curves of her projective buttocks.

Her hand fingers her detached eye with gentle precision as she blackens the lids.

Her over-all air of determined orientalism shows tigerish love while her smart sophistication reveals the supreme importance attached in her lovemaking to neatness of toilet.

•

He approaches her chamber.

Bearing a fly-whisk and a box of betelnuts, he leads her to the bed.

•

She is parted from her lover and driven to distraction by the enchantments of spring.

Alone with her desires, she strolls in a posh garden, holding in her hand a wand of candy flowers.

There is now a greater refinement in her body, a more conscious delight in feminine charm and gorgeous richness of philosophy.

•

Itching with love, she reclines on the terrace in the sultry stillness of a summer night.

Her whole posture suggests a state of restless longing, for which the only cure will be her lover's return.

Out of the dark trees jaguars glide to brush past her nude skin, which emits a glow like the sky's.

·

She is playing with him as if with a yo-yo—the boy, suspended from her finger, jerks nervously up and down in unison with her thoughts.

The ardent character of her brooding is suggested by the brilliant red of her dress.

·

An air of gentle tenderness marks their dalliance.

Her hand shyly strokes his wrist, a reticence implying the exquisite character of her feelings.

She moves on easy lights, lightly easing everyone over to the bed.

·

It is a little after dusk, the full moon just rising over rocky cliffs.

She stands holding a flower while a maid beguiles her with music from inside her vagina. A deer symbolizing the absent lover advances through the trees.

JIM CARROLL

The Distances

The accumulation of reefs
piling up one over the others
like thoughts of the sky increasing as the head rises
unto horizons of wet December days perforated
with idle motions of gulls . . . and our feelings.

I've been wondering about what you mean,
standing in the spray of shadows before an ocean
abandoned for winter, silent as a barque of blond hair.

and the way the clouds are bending, the way they "react"
to your position, where your hands close over your breasts
like an eyelid approving the opening of "an evening's light."

parasites attach themselves to the moss covering
your feet, blind Cubans tossing pearls across the jetty,
and the sound of blood fixes our eyes on the red waves.

                                        it is a shark!

and our love is that rusted bottle . . . pointing north,
the direction which we turn, conjuring up our silver knives
and spoons and erasing messages in the sand, where you wrote

"freezing in the arctic of our dreams," and I said
"yes" delaying the cold medium for a time
while you continued to "cultivate our possessions"

as the moon probably "continued" to cradle.
tan below the slant of all those wasted trees
while the scent carried us back to where we were:

dancing like the children of great diplomats
with our lean bodies draped in bedsheets and
leather flags while the orchestra made sounds

which we thought was the sky, but was only a series
of words, dying in the thick falsetto of mist.
for what can anyone create from all these things:

the fancied tilt of stars, sordid doves
burning in the hollow brick oven, oceans
which generalize tears, it is known to us

in immediate gestures, like candle drippings
on a silk floor. what are we going to do with anything?
besides pick it up gently and lay it on the breath

of still another morning, mornings which are
always remaining behind for one thing or another
shivering in our faces of pride and blooming attitude.

in the draught of winter air my horse is screaming
you are welcoming the new day with your hair leaning
against the sand, feet dive like otters in the frost

and the sudden blue seems to abandon as you leap. O
to make everything summer! soldiers move along lines
like wet motions in the violent shade's reappearance.

but what if your shadow no longer extends to my sleeping?
and your youth dissolves in my hand like a tongue, as
the squandered oceans and skies will dissolve into a single plane

(so I'll move along that plane)   unnoticed and gray
as a drift of skulls over the cool Atlantic where I am
standing now, defining you in perhaps, the only word I can.

as other words are appearing, so cunningly, on the lips
of the many strips of light. like naked bodies
stretched out along the only beach that remained,
brown and perfect below the descending of tides.

Maybe I'm Amazed

Just because there is music
piped into the most false of revolutions

it cannot clean these senses
of slow wireless death crawling
from a slick mirror
1/8th its normal size . . .

Marty was found dead by the man literally
blue 12 hours after falling out
at the foot of the Cloisters
with its millions in rare tapestry
and its clear view of the Hudson

and even testing your blue pills
over and over to reverse
my slow situations
I wind up stretched across the couch
still nodding with Sherlock Holmes
examining our crushed veins

Richard Brautigan,
I don't care who you are fucking
in your clean California air

I just don't care

though mine are more beautiful anyway
           (though more complex perhaps)

and we have white flowers too
right over our window on 10th St.
like hands that mark tiny x's
across infinity day by day

but even this crumb of life
I eventually surface toward
continues to nod as if I see you all
thoughtlessly
through a carefully inverted piece
of tainted glass

shattered in heaven
and found on these streets

Love Poem (Later)
for Rise

The little bonus
of my hand on your breast
makes a bus seem so useful
when some rain begins to open.

the cloud waves cracked sun shafts
when the sky began to whistle
and I was thinking about it all night
just watching it move from my eye to my hand.

it's not very meaningless
the changes one makes lying down
it's almost the way a mountain feels
when it becomes a star

BILL BERKSON

Sweet Lord
to Ted Berrigan

A slice of pumpernickel, mustard rare
      and sweet times turning of the night; in the depths
a bird flaps down near the corners
      of a book. It's his book—black
& white, he reads it, goes
               around in it, sighing tenderly
        in breeze, happy bird.
Yellow, blue, and litmus pink. Under the sky
      it's awful eating
   and singing all the time
            then day dawns & you
    see it's right, true
          it should be full
              & so should you

eating, singing, flying, reading
      & living here
          there for it
   to you beginning
    near, out, up, and around
  now
    Sweet Lord.

Vibration Society

It doesn't matter where I knew her.

We were star-explorers together.

Now it's lost.

The ocean lies some 200 yards away
in practically any direction.

Great gobs of devotion make me swallow
hard in the soft blonde chair. Into
the dragon! no one left out! Some fool
puts trees in front of his house in time
to see it all slip away into illusory
sludge. We gather our wits to save him,
but it's too late. Your beautiful
daughter learns the hard ways of wave
dwellers. We walk away smiling,
pink in foul sunset.

Twilight Time

in Bolinas
to Angelica Clark

The livelong days proceed in one
quick adjustable flow
                    as one now going goes
along as one
            to wonder, is
  this chronology?
                        In fact, one can think that
                &
          think again!
                        And that is *one*.
            a simple yes
                        or no in
the whirling mist
                of possibilities
                            between worlds
        & this is slow
                    it won't do
                    but
                    it will *be*long!

•

Heavenly shades of night are falling
around the place one turns toward
often.
   A short space away
        but really it's close
and comfort's there, to spare,
          its tender stays,
           there, with you

I'd go now, too
but I've been already
but I'll go again
     too
       & walking
    along straight, starlit roads:

Brighton, Terrace, Ocean Parkway, Grove
& Juniper, Kale,
Laurel, Maple, & on

down Cherry, a little ways up Nymph
         here to there
     the days are endless
though they surely go
        & soon
    it's twilight time
        now
        & in the years
     (but later, for *that*)

Following these ways
to find you there, I feel
I've gotten to this place
& that one's real

JOE BRAINARD

from *Bolinas Journal*

Friday, May 28th. Bolinas. A motel room. "Smiley's." Just had breakfast across the street. Very good French toast and bacon.

When I arrived in San Francisco yesterday afternoon Bill and Lewis were there to meet me. A good sight.

We drove around San Francisco a bit. (Really beautiful.) Had lunch. Went to City Lights. And then to Lewis's place. (Wine.) Where none of us knew exactly what we wanted to "do" so I suggested a drink in a bar.

Finding a parking place became a big ordeal but finally we did.

A Bloody Mary in a funny Hawaiian bar. (Right out of the movies.) With live music. With nobody in it except one drunk and us. Pretty weird.

Then we almost went to a movie until I realized that I was just in another big city and that what I really wanted was to be in the country. By the ocean. Bolinas. Where Bill lives.

Bill, by the way, is Bill Berkson. And Lewis is Lewis Warsh.

So Bill and I drove back to Bolinas where we had a few drinks at "Smiley's," the bar/motel I'm staying at now.

Last night in the bar a girl Bill and I were talking to especially stands out in my head. A "hippie" type. (Sorry, but that's what words are for.) Very sincere in what she believed in. But what she believed in was totally fucked up. But like I said, very sincere about it all.

It always bothers me, this combination. Of sincere *and* wrong. It doesn't seem fair. Sincere should always be right.

Pictures on my hotel room wall: a twin set of teeny-boppers twisting on the beach with giant heads and even more giant eyes.

The daisies really grow big around here. In big clumps. Like big bushes.

I can hear every sound the family in the next room is making.

Everyone said I was going to love Joanne Kyger and I do, *I do!*

Bolinas is more like I thought Jamaica would be than Jamaica was. (So lush.)

And *fantastic* flowers everywhere.

A lot of talk about things I don't know much about. Like eastern religions. Ecology. And local problems. Sewer system problems in particular. And people I don't know. Strange names continually pop up.

The Creeleys are great, Bob and Bobbie. I really do like both of them a lot.

A love possibly appears. Gordon Baldwin. Afraid to let myself be too optimistic tho. One thing in my favor is that this seems a very "straight" community. (Which means not much competition.) However—I don't even know if he's interested yet. Vibrations tell me "yes." But experience tells me not to expect anything until it happens. Always better to be surprised than disappointed. Which has nothing to do with anything because the truth of the matter is that I *am* going to be disappointed if nothing happens.

Lots of dogs.

Lots of dope.

Visions of falling madly in love with Gordon continue to grow in my head. Unrealistically, I know, but what can I do?

At the same time (now) I realize, tho, that I just want to fall in love with *somebody*. So I'm not sure, really, how much Gordon has to do with it. I mean, if it wasn't Gordon it would probably be someone else.

But then, I sometimes wonder if *wanting* to fall in love isn't just as important as *who* you fall in love with. (Just as important, I mean, towards helping it happen.) And perhaps even more so.

I don't know. To tell you the truth—I'll consider myself lucky just to get a little sex out of him.

Really especially crazy about Bob and Bobbie and Joanne. So nice how some people just turn you on instantly. And so nice to feel that you do them too.

Tom and Angelica Clark look great. And Juliet. Great and healthy and comfortable and satisfied. As tho they don't need anything. Or anyone. (Why isn't this more attractive to me than it is?) I certainly don't resent it. Maybe it's just that I don't see how I can fit into all this. (?)

A lot of being inside your own head here. A lot of talk about it. And a lot of talk about inside other people's heads too.

And a lot of talk about houses.

It seems to me that there is a lot to be said for "finding" yourself in your head, as opposed to "being" there.

Does that make sense? (I *think* so.)

I really do admire Bob Creeley. So much alive ("in" and digging) and really trying.

Trying is great. And knowing you are trying must be even greater. I think Bob does. (Know it.)

And if so, I hope he's proud of it. (Has the satisfaction of.)

I just rented a house for one month. Can't believe it. $250. I believe the $250. It's that I rented a house for a month that I can't believe. So much for "seeing" California. Well—I'm not a very good traveler anyway. I like a clean shirt every morning. And work. I really need to work a lot. And that's hard to do when you're moving around. (And when there's Gordon).

Tomorrow I move out of the Creeley house and in with Gordon for one night. (Until June 1st when I move into my own place.) A totally obvious move on my part, moving in with Gordon for one night, as I could just as easily stay with Bob and Bobbie one more night. I wonder what Gordon thinks about *that*.

Gordon's house. Late afternoon. Just moved in. (Well, I walked through the door carrying my little suitcase and sat down.) We talked a bit, Gordon and I, about nothing in particular, and then he said he had to go out and look for a rock. A rock to *do* something with. Didn't quite catch what. At any rate, that's where Gordon is now.

Obviously I make him nervous. Maybe this is a good sign.

I really don't feel optimistic tho. (You just keep telling yourself that, Joe.)

But I do feel optimistic about being able to do some good work here. And being able to relax more here. And take things as they come more here.

I'm tired of fighting life. I'd just like to sink in a bit and get cozy.

Really don't know why I push myself so. God only knows life is short enough without rushing through it.

Gordon is still looking for a rock I guess.

Guess I'll go shave.

It wasn't easy, but we *did* finally end up in the same bed together last night. (Just messed around a bit tho, as we were both pretty stoned.) Well, in the same bed for *part* of the night. Until Gordon couldn't sleep so he ended up on the sofa. ("The caffeine of Pepsi.") Likely story.

Gordon *did* imply that we should get together again, but I think he was just being nice.

Maybe he's afraid he might get "stuck" with me for a whole month if he gets involved.

Or maybe he likes to confine his love/sex life to San Francisco. (This *is* a small town.)

Or maybe I just don't turn him on.

Well—I tried.

I like my new house. On Terrace Road. Half way up the mesa. Nice view of the ocean. (Through some wires.) But already I don't even notice them. Inside the house is pretty plain. (Normal.) With lots of orange. And some Mexican stuff. Right next door that *I Hate to Cook* lady lives. And two houses down is a house Isadora Duncan danced in once.

And it's always nice to know you can take a loud shit without feeling self-conscious about it. (Should the occasion arise.)

And it's the only way I can be totally relaxed. (Damn it.) To be alone.

The sun isn't out today but, today, I don't really care.

If it's possible to feel good and bad at the same time that's how I feel today. And I do. So I guess it is.

This is a great place, Bolinas, but it isn't for me now.

Everything I fear that will someday catch up with me, would catch up with me too fast here. Like the "why" of art. And the "I give up" of finding love and happiness.

That's pretty corny, I know, to believe that love and happiness can be "found." But I guess I do. (Especially when I don't think about it I do.)

And I guess it's pretty corny to be proud of being corny. But I guess I am.

Bolinas is such a basic place. *The land* being so important. Survival seems to be the main issue.

But for me life is still very much a matter of day and night. Can't think much beyond that. And I don't *want* to.

I guess I'm not tired of playing games yet.

Or maybe I'm just afraid of what will be left if I ever do.

And maybe, just maybe, that's good. (Good, I mean, for me.)

ALICE NOTLEY

Six Phoebe Poets:
A Little Anthology

PHOEBE SLEEP

Phoebe: a baby
Asleep and sleeping with her
The chickens: asleep
The carrot: a pillow
Lettuce: have sleep
Sleep: allow her
Some sleep: Ocean asleep

(Kenneth Koch)

PHOEBE MILK

Milk is bigger—half-a-gallon, at least—
pick it up and the milk moves, rising
enthusiastically below the neck, heavy as
a breast, she brings home the milk in a
bandana.

(James Schuyler)

PHOEBE FLOOR

On the paper mat the sassies
Cloistered, the Phoebe floor was marked
Near the 18 boots and the city
Of unmitigated feet—no wan ending
Of the trail among mud.

(John Ashbery)

PHOEBE SASS

    plumb   lic   hose

         dives

marls pais loops watts

  lock mix deem

           meat bubble

(Clark Coolidge)

PHOEBE LIGHT

The great cosmetic

Strangeness of the normal deep person

(Tom Clark)

PHOEBE NOVEMBER

I leap
in my cups.

(Ron Padgett)

Written on purpose
by Alice Notley
for Phoebe MacAdams's Birthday, Nov 14/71

JOHN DOSS

Birth

I was called
called. and I go 30 miles to the city

called to ATTEND
A birth
Attend ! To learn, be at attention

Now

Birth: a new beginning
Labor of Love
A child
Joy ! Joy !

Attend ! Not to do anything,
Be there,
To be.

A waiting, vigil, gathering of the clan
Ancient family function.
Natural home event
Celebration
Re-affirmation

Myself affirmed.

Let me too you how it is being—
To be: physician,
medicine man
Shaman
myself.

Attend !

There she is ! Dig Her !

Squatting, primitive, like at stool
Lower back abut a kitchen door jamb
Leaning
Flat footed
Legs spread
Knees bent
Hands clasped into knees / fingers spread
Hunched shoulders
Arms straight from neck to knee
Laboring, facing East in prayer
Her lines forming a triangle
Enclosing a circle of gravid belly
Magic symbols.

Woman. Small bones, ruffed reddish hair
whisping about face
She / blowing at it.

S-curving from small head
around neck / tangle over filled breasts

Freckled sweat / you shine

Your eyes / Eyes you are in your eyes
You turn out to see yourself

And I in turn / see myself
Tell me who I am / I will tell *you* who you are.

Who's in charge around here?

She is !

Laboring mother / Doing the woman thing

I touch her with my eyes
We encompass each other
and I watch with compassion

With black bag, mostly empty
A knife, gold pen, paper, string, key
Odds and ends of my identity
But mostly I came as myself

My hands, naked before
your divine act

It's your thing / do it well
I say to you

We have work to do
and I settled down to comprehend
and learn.

What is going on?
A family thing
Celebration
Tribal act / old
As all time

The clan has gathered
Chief, minstrels, poets
Wizards, pilgrims, midwives

The sexual smell of birth fills the air.

Gathering together
To witness, affirm
Attend
again

Is anyone there to witness ?

(family)   Joan   mother
               Billy Batman   father
               oldest child, male, Jade
               next oldest, male, Hassan
               youngest (not for long), female, Caledonia

Women:

(attending)   Lenore Kandel, poet

Cassandra, witch

Sam, Peter's girl

Helene, gypsy wife of printer Claude

Female child of Helene, and 6 months

Sara, wife of John, pilgrim from Denver

Woman, neighbor with blanket

Men:

(watching)   Emmett Grogan, Digger

Kirby Doyle, poet

Richard Brautigan, poet

Claude Hayward, printer, Digger

Peter Cohan, mime trouper

Gandalf, white wizard

John Glaser, husband of Sara (pregnant)

Billy Fritsch, Lenore's man

Others:

Obstetrician & Male Nurse

Poets, beggars, minstrels, chief

Gypsies, Indians,

Pilgrims,

Children of their time

Diggers

Vision of poverty

All in a pad / boxed wooden tepee

Family love,

Surrounded by tribal love

Chiefs, shaman, witches, magic makers

Godfathers, Godmothers.
Are all there to love, an orgy of
deliverance.

—to put ceremony where it also belongs
in the most elementary of human acts

That's who's there—

and I

The men mostly watch, squat shadows
cross-legged on the floor
Doing men talk and things

The women
Attended
The mother to be

Whelping, man can only watch
Can he feel it ?
Total earth mother mystery
Does he know ?
The mystery

Olson said:

Whatever is born or done this moment of time
has the qualities of this moment in time

What happened this moment of time ?

We were all there
Not here,
There in that (this) moment of time
Each one to himself (herself)
Responding to the moment
of magic
a birth

a waiting, stillness, expectancy
vibrant.

Family / Family sounds
Eating
Laughing
Talk about what's new ?
This is what's new:
Compassion, concern for

JOAN

The center of a living mandala

Connected to each other
Connected, wired, re-connected
Bonded
Glued, un-glued
Cosmic glue of synchronicity
No place

The women attended
Held you
Rubbed where it hurt
Feeling, skin to skin
Feeling (pick up) your work and Joy

You labored hard and long on the kitchen floor
Feet to the West, setting sun,
crouched around with midwives
Handmaidens.
Nothing spoken, your needs
Attended

We talked of births and afterbirths
cutting cords, biting them free
like primitives do.
No, not that, but would you if
necessary. I know
You know

Joan you and I talked—
Explored each other,
liked what we found.

Your particulars—young healthy
Fourth pregnancy. Three if hospitals
Quick labors except for one

A hang up—occiput posterior
Sometimes requires assistance,
Cold metal, called forceps.

Bag of water unbroken—
Pains (?) Contractions regular.
If you were in pain it seemed
a kind of ecstasy to watch.

You chose your position—
I did not change it.
Do your thing where it's
most comfortable for you.

Did you want to go to a hospital?
No ! At home—where you are.
For your family and tribe

So. / OK / let's see what happens.

Not much happening,
not much to do—
Play with children—
open black bag
Gifts for children
Key to Hassan, paper for Jade
String tied to Caledonis

Quiet late afternoon
In the country I would hum with bees

Quiet late afternoon
In the city cars hiss and buses
Rumble and fart
making a shambles of thought

Restless / Do something !
Find quiet
an empty room, disarray of children activity
Tarot cards everywhere
Must be neat with destiny
I gather, pick each card
Arrange them, cast aside.
Forgotten this (that) moment

There were other things there
to do. Prepare for the cutting
of cord
Knife pocket piece
My knife
Hard clean steel clasped in green jade
Dull from non-use

Sharpened with found Moroccan coin
inscribed with triangle, stars
Arap writing, Sanskrit
without over bars.
Silver and steel
worked back and forth
to and fro / a sharpening
edging
Finally, sharp
It dragged across my thumbnail
Tasted on tongue
Had Joan touch blade to mouth

The coin I carried in my mouth
Asked all to touch or kiss
this coin.

Now sitting near your head
children laying about
Playing, knew something
Special was going on
But still hungry as children are.

An orange, peeled by cutting with knife.
Circling the top
contra navel, then,
quartering
Holding it up for the children to see
Peeled
Four quarters
A circle.
Juice trickles down chin
Children laugh.

Later near time of birth
Cassandra, cross-legged, facing South
Reads the cards, telling
of this time.

Arranged by whom   ?
Children scattered cards,
Random, unwanted, unbelieved   ?
Gathered by me without thought.

I just wanted to keep the cosmos in order.
Sam cast them, Celtic cross
Cassandra reads with open mind
"Do they tell of the future of this
yet to be born child?" I asked

You said, 'Strong, yeah strong reading
Good signs"
Your eye averted, unlike you,
Cassandra.
What did you see that you did not want
to tell?
Did you doubt the cards?
It was, after all, a reading for everyone
in this moment.

Did it make you want to love us more?
Or in despair, unwanted, unbidden,
did you see the future as past?

Sitting in the corner, near the men.
Idly moving gold pen over
paper in Billy's guest book.

Images of black bats, wings, craps
Numbers   4   July
               5
               6
               7
swirls, connecting, unconnected

mindlessness taking form
Indian shaman painting sand
Black / White
No color
yet.

No immediate use
for doodling now

Later, always later
Placental blood rubbed
into book.
Certification that the circled 5 July has
been noted in '67
Black / White / Red
all one

Hot July night, stripped to the waist
Bare footed
Clean diaper in left hand
I washed
Washing hands is prayer
Facing North, Joan on my right
Table lamp on floor lights the scene
Blessed hot running water.
Soap. Palms together
In and out, around, up the wrists

My hands were clean
Cleaned, cleansed

Pink and alive
More alive each time I touched you.

Too long, 12 long hours
for you.
Bag of waters unbroken
Baby way over on right
side. Feel mostly legs,
lumpy in your belly.
Wincing each time the wave
of bunching muscle crosses,
courses, downward
Mucous "show" hours ago
Finally you tire, nap
Contractions less intense.
Inertia gone—a hang
up. What?

Something wrong.

I must examine you
inside.
Gentle, easy
"Like love making" I said
Not rape

Rosette of engorged hemorrhoids
gently returned.
Fingers far up—Bulging
membrane, sac of water
Fills your open cervix

Baby almost
floating away from finger.

Rupture membranes, speed
Labor. No tools, finger
nails clipped short, won't work
Muttered aloud, "I wish I
had a kocher" John
reaches in tote bag
Produces a 'kocher'—his roach holder
A real life saver.
Crotch linked, long toothed
pick up.

Not sterile ! / Heat it ! / dammit !

Kirby fires it over kitchen burner
to glowing white, red
Hissing hot. Little white sparks
Flow from its tip

Cooled in warm water
to body heat.
Chrome steel / soft vaginal flesh
Slid along fingers to bulging
bag (amniotic sac)
Open teeth / push / grasp / pull—
                    That breaks the caul!
Shit!
Gushing fluid, brownish,
washes over my hand.

Trouble, fetal trouble
fetal distress it's called
Fecal staining of amniotic
Fluid

Stop—Attention.
Attend, must hurry

Head easily felt now
Look (feel) for landmarks.
Sutures
fontanelle—
coronal ridge, sagittal
lambdoidal ridge—
Big hole up / little hole down

A hang up
Occiput posterior
Face up / sunny side up
The head must rotate almost half circle
for easy birth.

Cervix open, head
engaged, membranes
broken,
first stage (of labor) complete
Enter stage two.

Baby in distress
Does the mother know?

Everything stops.
hand over your heart
Eyes locked we
consult each other.
Transmit concern.
Hold down fear.
Easy.
Your heart steady
Easy does it.

Need help—an instrument
(like long fingers) to grasp
head for turning.

I send Peter
He returned with another doctor, (and a male nurse)
white coat, white eyes
eyes the scene

Wants out,
Doesn't dig it.
Plastic gloves, examines,
GONE !

Leaving nothing
almost as if he hadn't been there
He looked at me, I look at him
Words pass.
STAY ! PLEASE HELP !
Be a doctor!

No contact
He is gone.

Now a rising fear that
all may be lost
Abstract civilized fear
Put it down !
Be yourself
Attend !

Back to Joan

On hand and knees before you
Fingers reaching, stretching. (Lenore is there)
Hands on belly
Straining to turn baby about
You are now clasped between my hands.
I feel you push, strain
Push down

Head now in vagina
we all look to see the crowning
Labia opening, bulging.
It cannot be stopped now.

Head almost out
Perineum stretching
Glass thin, transparent.
Hold back, gently.
Next push should do it.
"Here, bite the coin" I said. You did.

Head now partly over
stretched taut opening.

Now
Push
Push Come
Easy baby
Up and over

Orgasmic push
Grunt
anus open round mouth
Watery floppy sound
Head free
in my hands

Face down
Home free.

Shoulders slip easily
Then the body
with Billy now there
Holding him.

It's a boy !
He cries

Cord in hand
silver shiny spiral
blue.

Alive with pulsations
Snake-like writhing

Pulsations stop
Abruptly
Tie with nylon cord
tie again
Double tie, square knots
with granny keeper.
Trim excess string
Give to Billy
Knife, jade, small sharp blade.

Cut
splatter of blood
Baby free
Loving hands everywhere
Laid on mother's breast.
Cord hanging loose at vagina.

I hear shouts—his name

Digger!
Digger Batman
He is born
Born free
I gave him the coin from my mouth

Slow deep shudders envelope you.   Gandalf gives the
Subsiding orgasm of birth   time 10:41
Culmination of conception

Conclusion of the beginning
Letting out
Release
Second stage complete

Tension leaves the group.
Spent
Wait for expulsion of placenta

Placenta: Selfless product of conception
          The giver / taker
          Now that God has done his work
          It does away with itself
          Born as an afterthought
          To be buried in the S.E. corner
          of the village
          Hopi fashion.

That organ / parasite
Neither mother nor child
Intermediary, middle man
Hormone factory,
Feeder
Sucker
A life of its own, yet
no conscious life
or does it?
First to be there
Last to leave
Spirit

Gentle tugs at cord
Then a sliding easy
Expulsion.
Soft
Meaty
Liverish disc Warm blood
Slippery

Call for basin
Afterbirth placed in it
meaty side up

I ask all to touch
Flesh
Blood and
                    Taste.

Labor complete—3rd stage finished
Someone lights a dime store
Brass pipe of hash—
passed around—
it tasted of burnt flowers

Black woman, white eyes
living cave painting, small
In and out of the group
Ghostly in dim light offered a blanket, greyish old.
Not for the infant but to be
gently rubbed against the
receding empty uterus.

Sara used it
One of the last things I did was
check the uterus
There it was.

I put on my shirt, coat, sandals, pack
my bag and go home to Bolinas.

RICHARD BRAUTIGAN

Formal Portrait

I like to think of Frankenstein as a huge keyhole
and the laboratory as the key that turns the lock
and everything that happens afterward as just the
    lock turning.

Wood

We age in darkness like wood
and watch our phantoms change
   their clothes
of shingles and boards
for a purpose that can only be
   described as wood.

Shellfish

Always spend a penny
as if you were spending a
    dollar
and always spend a dollar
as if you were spending
a wounded eagle and always
spend a wounded eagle as if
you were spending the very
    sky itself.

Mouths That Kissed
in the Hot Ashes of Pompeii

Mouths that kissed
in the hot ashes of Pompeii
    are returning
and eyes that could adore their beloved only
in the fires of Pompeii
    are returning
and locked bodies that squirmed in ecstasy
in the lava of Pompeii
    are returning
and lovers who found their perfect passion
in the death of Pompeii
    are returning,
and they're letting themselves in
again with the names of your sons
and your daughters.

Pity the Morning Light
That Refuses to Wait for Dawn

Pity the morning light that refuses to wait for dawn
and rushes foolishly with its mercury pride to challenge
a responsibility that knows only triumph and gently bends
the stars to fit its will and cleans up afterwards all
that poor wasted light, leaving not a trace behind.

TED BERRIGAN

Things to do in Bolinas

                    Unlimber
                    Stretch
                    Listen :

                                      Stones
    Smoke   Beatles
                                    Kinks

             Groove on Angelica
                  & on Juliet

                        •

        Swallow (acid)
          two or three times

                    Country Pie

                      •

       Watch the natives suffer

                      •

dig the Recent Philip Whalen Past

scene

smile at Tom

Freeze & sleep

•

Fuck

•

Stroll along the edge
of the land

day & night

totally different

•

Take a long walk

a short drive

•

Read: Poetry

•

Eat
        Everything

                                        •

        Yearn for city lights

                                    •

drop out: drop in
                        for quiet tea
                        w/
                            Jack & Ebbe

                                •

            chat like a nut

        w/ Shau   he's a gas

                                •

Gas up   Shake

            Split

GAILYN SAROYAN

Poem for Strawberry

You can turn the pages
while Mommy changes
you.

One Bit of Gossip

One bit of gossip—yesterday we passed Brautigan walking down the hill we were walking up (he owns a house in Bolinas furnished only with a bed, chair and table apparently which he never lives in, but rather stays in his one-room San Francisco apartment cluttered with memorabilia—or so the Story goes). It was the first time we'd seen him around. *In Watermelon Sugar* was written in Bolinas—there's a place further up the hill that smells just like watermelon 'sugar' after the rain in the sun, which I mention to Aram and he said 'Oh he wrote that book in Bolinas.'

Haiku

Strawberry
waters the flowers
in her hand

.

Hitch-hiking

—"If a car comes, put up your thumb."
—"No. You do it."

Strawberry's Love Song

"Hold my hand
Pat my hand
Kiss my little hand."

Poem to the Moon

Light
at night.

Poem

Andrew's
Leather
Glasses

From A Diary

Strawberry is drinking her tea after breakfast and watching me while I draw her. I drew the eyes—"I see Strawberry!" she said, jumping up; and then decided to settle down and finish her tea.

While I finished the drawing and started to write this she went over to her little toy drawer and pulled out her calico heart I made for her and said "I'm reading my heart"—holding it up like an open book in front of her.

JOHN THORPE

I Just Lost My Tension Again

I walk around with no ideals or goals. I pass ripe blackberry bushes.

There's a man in me who would prove. He is right but little else. My knowledge of people was built up somewhere else. It was a heavy handed preparation and it dies hard.

I blew money. I lost things. I got over the loud things for a while. Loud or quiet is about the same. It means you don't have anything to come on to people with. And you have to give up first.

I feel like everybody knows but me. I just sit there openmouthed.

Yesterday I watched heavily environmental faces: half-closed faces with smiles that carry into the skull. I decided I just don't want to see anyone.

There are the people to hold in my arms. There is the street.

There is a laugh that indicates simply I drink and I'm too afraid to pay attention.

There is a lupine bush. It's somehow the fact I don't move alone.

My boots are starting to wear down on the side, they're lop-sided so the heel juts out. It's the inhibition of physical flaw I feel before I hear talk.

I did very little. I had a central character by virtue of that. Not as if Id found a place they couldn't take away.

I did what I wanted. And I brought two children into this world. I respected the mystery and mastered nothing I'm aware of.

I squat here, looking at the moon, deciding to appear.

September

I went out to add to the old compost heap, but the goat was tangled in the clothesline. Each rung of the chain had gotten under another rung of chain & it had all balled up. So I untangled it and pulled it out of her hooves & from around her legs. Then gave her a bowl of chow. The chickens saw the bowl of chow & ran over, so I clucked at em & led em to the shed where I dumped out the last of the scratch. Then I went in the house & got a sack of mash, brought it out back and made em piles. By this time the sun was out. I took the goat down to the marsh & chained her to a 12 foot ladder. Then I went back to the packing case & started turning compost. The hay looked pretty good. I turned the manure over on top & pulled out the stalks and vines. Then I needed topsoil. I looked around for the shovel. Not out front. Not by the fence. I looked in the shed & back of the garden. I went back to the compost pile & the chickens were standing in it. I needed to cover the pile. There was chicken wire in the shed but I couldn't find wire clippers. Then I passed the rabbit hutch & saw the rabbits on their hind legs. I remembered there were no more pellets so I went behind the coops & pulled out an armful of rib grass & put it in with the mother white rabbit. Then I went to the shed & got gunny sacks, went back to the compost pile, kicked the chickens out & laid the burlap over the pile. Then I went into the kitchen & asked Rene if she knew where the shovel was. She said she loaned it to Scott Wilson 2 days ago.

Tonight I saw the Canadian gypsy weaving down Wharf Rd. with his violin. He just got out of jail, & said: "They couldn't make me think I was wrong."

Capt. Hammond built the 1st sawmill in 1851, sold it the next year to another Capt. the name of Allen. G.R. Morris built the second

mill & bought out the first. Meanwhile, Russians were still working
the lime kilns. I wonder what Ed Genazzi's grandparents were doing—
dairying? It's amazing how much Bruce Warring's old house next to
the school looks like the old Briones home in photos.

I'd like to invent a kind of sourdough starter that makes a kind
of bread or curd or even rennet or of something that can be grown
in the back yard. Also like to invent a substance as strong as steel that
could be projected or sprayed fast enough to dam a river.

Downtown started with George H. Gavitt buying from the
government—I don't quite understand how—160 acres at the point. He
built a wharf, saloon & hotel—a small wharf. And this happened—

1862—John Gifford's Hotel

1865—Ball at Petroleum Hotel, kept by Mr. Lacy
Ball at hotel of Don Jesus Alcaras to commemorate
Mexican independence.
Mr. Rosenberg acquired warehouse, post office & saloon

1868—Crane's Hotel

1869—Buckeye House

1898—Flagstaff Inn (formerly Bayveiw House)
Accommodates 40 guests. Rate $2 per day, $12 per week
Children under 10 half rates, Nurses $9 per week

1906—Earthquake demolished all waterfront bldgs.

I'm interested in this: you & me
Sometimes I'll summon up a large world
but god knows I'm not whizzing thru
on the seat of a ten-speed or followable
"self" more than a knuckle to suck on
watching kids run down the road holding their
pants up

"I have to go to the D.A.'s office and sign a warrant for him."

"A warrant? You mean you just told them his name?

"Well, I had to say something. If I said I didn't know who the father was, I could just hear them start lecturing me about contraception."

"But it's still a lousy thing to do."

"Oh they only check in the county. I think he's in L.A. I got one check and a box for the kids with his parent's house as the return address."

"How come you couldn't give the welfare a phony name?"

"They could've told."

"You could've given them the name of someone who's dead!"

"Look, *I didn't*, that's all, I just didn't."

      Ramona Briones   b. San Diego 1803

      Gregario Briones   b. Monterey 1797

> "with the exception of some few who had land
>   difficulties with him
>   he did not have an enemy in the world"

Now one of the hitches is that the cost of getting water & utilities to the watershed land between Bolinas & Stinson would be about a billion dollars. That's what's stopping some developer from moving in. (On the old county master plan this space is slated to hold 12 thousand people.)

Just after 12 noon I get a fearful feeling & I want to get *busy* but am sunk. Photos of the old town in Mrs. Jenkins scrapbook. Particularly Alfred Denby Easkoot, the county surveyor from 1853-71. Also, Chicken Charlie, 1907, and the Briones women sitting on the porch. The spaces between houses & mesas in back are huge. In 1866 there seem to have been 2 houses on Brighton, with a cattle grate across the road. The young boys wearing hats snapped as they walked across them.

This morning or last night a dog killed a duck & the kids found it. A huge gash was gone from its back but I thought we could eat the breast legs & wings. I put it in boiling water & plucked it for an hour. There were hundreds of nascent quills I didn't get out. Then I cut it open from the ass to the belly & gutted it. The kids watched. I opened it to the lungs & there were little maggots already, so I cut away the sides from the rib cage & 1 good leg—washed & wrapped them, & threw the rest to the chickens.

It's
about a man sitting on a coke crate, trouble with his father
lost a half days pay, made a dollar phone call
not on the way up but growing in ability
daughter pregnant, the other kids playing
in ferns along deer trails
Cigarettes moving along a drain ditch
Muggy night, broken home, a far-off plane
and the autumn California moon
with no stage or mocking person or
even mad horsemen left

Now this town has a thousand people. At about 5,000 people there begins to be shopping centers, drug stores, barbershops, etc. This vector that wants to move from the 1,000 now to the 5,000 people is occurring right now from week to week and not just in flashes.

with a 6 moth subscription
the Bulletin is selling lots in a
New Summer Resort

on Bolinas Beach
for $69.50
        or payable $9.50 down
and $3.00/month

        Privileges incl. use of Bath House
        Membership in the Club House
        Use of Shore Front Park.

        Bolinas is a 2nd landscape, the duck
        left of the six
        ducks

    "The thing about wanting to meet new people (chomp,
chomp) has to do (chomp) with inventing (chomp). You meet a new
person (chomp) you don't have to (chomp) invent the way you have
to (gulp) with people you've known a long time. Ah that tastes ok. So
parties are like (chomp) where people are trying to find a new person
to tell something to (chomp chomp chomp) that they couldn't tell to
someone else (chomp gulp swallow) or that they've tried to tell and
failed (swallow swallow ah). Or they want to tell it again (cough) to
someone who'll (cough) understand. You see?"

"WEEKEND"

    "On Friday I went downtown and saw Blair with Frankie.
And then the tide was going out and then we went under the houses
down through a bunch of gooshy mud and slippery mud and Blair
found this place by the rocks that you could slide in the mud on. And
then we went to this place where there was this sunken boat and then
Blair started running. And then when he stopped he started sliding.

And then I ran my fastest and stopped and I skidded for about half a mile. And then while I was skidding Blair was running after me and I turned while I was skidding and then Blair skidded right into the water. And then Blair went right home. But he stopped because he saw raccoon tracks all over the place. And then he got scared and he started running and I tried warning him. Then he stopped because there was a board covered with mud that he would go flying through the air if he went over it. And he went over it and he went flying back in to the water and then when he hit the water he started water skiing because he was going so fast a little bit and then he skied right onto Kent Island. And then he had to go all the way down to the other end of Kent Island to get back. And when he got there he said he'll never go over to that place again. But he said he's going to share what he did. And then I saw Dave at his house and was playing with Eric Jordan and they were out in a dinghy. Then I went back home.

Then on Saturday I watched most of the cartoons. Then I had to go to Cub Scouts, but they weren't open so I went down to Jesse's and then I saw Jesse there. We went up the creek and saw a salmon. Then we went up a little farther and we saw an undertow and a big waterfall. I threw a stick in and it went down the waterfall and it got smashed and then Jesse rolled a big tree in and when it went down all the branches went flying in the air because it broke on the rocks. And Jesse fell in but he didn't go down the waterfall because it was a little too shallow.

And on Sunday my dad came over and we went down to the cliffs and we jumped and we went up to the slides and I was scared to slide down at first but then I had to and I didn't like it so I just started jumping everyplace. The I jumped about 20 feet off the ground and I couldn't breathe for a second because I don't know why. And then I didn't want to jump that far anymore because it hurted on my chest. And then Hankie when he jumped he flipped and then I went down to the beach and then Hank jumped head-first into the water. But he had his diving mask on and his air tanks and his wet suit and he had all the skindiving equipment a man always uses and they were all in his size and so did I. And we went out into the ocean to look for little fishes and catch them in our nets and bring them back home. I caught a shark and Hankie caught a little baby salmon."

(Chris talking to Deetje)

Night drinking out on the street—guys slapping palms and laughing. "Evbody knows theres 2 kindsa people the quick & the dead hee hee hee." 3 guys from the commune & one slightly younger guy from Salt Lake City who'd given one of em a lift back to California. At some point one of the commune guys called him a good cat—he said "Thank you"—this made them crack up, someone being that polite!

Jill told me about a 3 day horseback trip she took around Lake Ranch.

I'm
classically
educated too

but
stuff
happened

Jim Stoops & I cut 4 large limbs from th cypress trees out front. it looks like a cord of wood. Used the green needley branches around the base of Dick's fence where the slope needs retention. I started to deadwood the trees—did the lower 20 feet of one. It'll take months. It's kinda scary, the yard full of dry wood & a warm northern wind—brushfire time of year. There's a water shortage: 5 million gallons left in the reservoir til the rains come.

Midafternoon I went downtown and got a quart of beer. Gail Schwering was sitting in the back of the vacant lot where the Greyhound buses park. She was selling her household stuff. Sitting dressed in a white petticoat & scarf with rings on her fingers & drinking a cup of soup. The ridge from there was between a red bush and a green bush. She told a dream—that she & a lover flew silently over Bolinas & she was cold til they got to the one place where a ledge of cloud persistently stays on the ridge north of Stinson—& when they there they sat on it & were no longer cold. She made $10.

> Sitting back of Pepper's
> "They sure got a lot of
>   garbage back here
>   You oughtta move down a
> little—it really stinks here"

The goat ate the apple tree. This is that interesting thing: the world is never either/or. I can't hurt the goat. I won't kill the rabbits under the house until they're big enough to feed us all. In the meantime they eat the garden. So it goes. When the kids take a bath, the ground by the septic tank trickles in a black stream. The Water Department guys are shouting at each other, & Kit's crying cause he can't find a chair high enough to cop a pack of my matches.

Kit got a dollar thru the mail, & on the first day of school he & Stefano & I went downtown in the morning to the store. Kit gave Stefano fifty cents & they each got a popsicle for 10 cents. Then we went to the dock. While Stefano was playing he accidentally dropped a dime thru the crack in the wharf timbers. He was sad but Kit immediately took his dime out and dropped it thru the same crack.

Now I don't understand this world of magnified troubles.
I bring water to the duckhouse.
I kick the dog out of the way.
I don't know the ropes, & shall henceforth
never mention 'them'

I dreamed of a green man of stable shape. This shape was a double key.
It could fit the stars.

"What are you guys doing?"
"Oh, solving the world's problems . . . "

BILL BROWN

A Scenario

The Old Woman: *Salome Booth*
The Girl: *Angelica Clark*
The Voice & the Poet: *Joanne Kyger*
Camera: *Philip Greene, Bill Brown*

the old woman   *the viola*
     blue air   *(heavy slow gentle)*
     street water   *like old chants*
     her shoes   *like slow exhalation*
     the black coat
     the cane

     (abrupt fade)

alone on a narrow street
     white light behind her   *children street voices*
     children stare quickly

     cars wooshing

she's gone

she walks in winter sunlight
  by the vegetable crates
   big winter melons   *metal strikes metal*
   the Chinese words

she looks at the shop window   *truck engine*
  words on the window
  a street on the window

            (Joanne's voice)
the girl's face & wild mustard

            From this moment
the girl's gone   *and hence backward*

the old woman behind the window   *(echo: from this moment*
   she seems to gaze down   *and hence backward)*
   behind reflections
burlap   *a visitation*
a truck passes
an old man passes   *(echo: and hence backward)*
she puts out her hand

      echoes through the apparent opening
      of the tomb

the large gold mushroom
the black soil on the stem
she touches the mushroom
   the Chanterelle *the narrow passage is the mind's reasoning*
   she gazes down   *is the mind's reasoning*
   the slow gaze   *in clarity*
   the slow hands   *as she moves like a shadow*

the girl is walking up the hill
    the wind
    the shaking weeds   *like a shadow*
    white lace shawl on her shoulders   *having lived her life before*
                                  it is now the particular graces

the Chanterelle   *that surface*
    turning in her old hand
her shoulders bent forward   *(8 lines above are voices*
& holding the white skirt   *multiplied back on themselves)*
she glides
Queen Anne's lace
long stalks   *running*
puffball lights
thistles flaring   *running (soft)*
her mouth opened
she isn't smiling   *that is not lighter than spring*

the hand the Chanterelle
    old lowered eyes   *(the echo voices go*
                                away to
she comes down under dark trees   *one voice*
    & lines of sunlight   *one echo*
    & she kneels on the stream   *quavers, lost*
    & sits near the ferns   *in*
                                its echo)

the Chanterelle under the ferns
    & she picks the mushroom
    & turns it in her fingers
    she lifts it to her cheek

the old eyes don't move   *water*

she walks in the stream   *water (soft)*
    the bare feet splash in light
    she holds the mushroom

                                    is revealed
she's taking the mushroom
    from the grocer's hand   *as the female*
    she gives him money   *opens out*
    she leaves the shop   *to receive*
                          her own death

the girl walks fast through bright grass

                             which is her own

the woman walks up the street slowly

                             eternal youth

the girl walks fast

                             her own love of herself

the white hair in the blue street
                    (echo)
the girl jumps on smooth rocks
    the stream is around the rocks   *her own love of herself*
                    (echo)
the street water glistens

                             her own love of herself

flaring sunlight & white insects
    she moves down the stream   *(echo fades)*
                        her own love of herself

she walks to her room
    the cane on the wet street   *(Joanne's voice melts*
    her shoes on the wet street   *lost under the hissing*
                        wind which goes on

the waves, white froth, black rocks
the girl's face   *& the children yelling far off*
the face's gone   *noises of a pool room from its*
wind   *opened door*
wild mustard weeds

                          the wind's hissing

The Gardeners

Still milk clouds on the mountain, wind in the south, purple first light.
Maybe rain. Good omens I said. Thinking about this star magnolia,
what a young tree, branchlets covered in white flowers in this purple
first light . . .

What happened here was 6 of us going double time inside 500 square
ft with 6 shovels, 4 picks, 2 dig bars, block & tackle & sideplanks plus
assorted blocks & chocks, one power auger for the plant holes, 25 flats
of dichondra & bronze ajuga, 3 rock cotton-easters, 3 jasmines the
wrong kind for this place, a couple dogwood trees, a lot of smaller stuff
for around the rocks like pen stemmons and leriopes & tiger grasses
etc., also a ton & ½ of place stones which's about 8 or so stones & one
guy has a hangover & keeps running to the faucet & one guy's talking
about the woman who just sawed another woman into 8 pieces & stole
her head, & one guy wants a raise & keeps swearing pretty loud &
everybody's running in circles & sweating & in about 3 hours it starts
to look like something that goes under the name of Japanese garden in
these parts & the lady we're working for tells me to move the dogwood
& everybody's out of breath and the boss's happier than a sonofabitch
because we're done before noon & going out the gate I looked over
my shoulder surprised because that star magnolia was still white with
a little February sunlight on it, it was still there I mean, it hadn't gone
away, in fact it didn't even know about us, & we went to another big
lady's house the other side of the county & began digging a lot of holes
in the ground . . . .

KEITH LAMPE

An Editorial

Should whaling ships be blown up to save our few remaining whales, noble wise brother & sister mammals? Well, we should not try such hazardous things till we have carefully prepared for the experience of our *own* deaths. Without such preparations, our deaths are unnatural and therefore bad karma. Preparation for death in our inherited culture is usually a slow process because we have no forms for it. There is an important distinction between preparing for death and taking a death trip. If we do get kilt during some transformational act, it just goes to show that nobody's perfect. The possibility anyway of "bliss apocalypse." We all have our lives ahead of us. A nice time to be had by all. Hemp. "We are all becoming religious again," is a way to say it. Fearless in new forms. "Nothing can happen to us that does not belong to us in our innermost being." The politics of visvavajra. The return of the great white whale, "who has never really left us."

STEPHEN RATCLIFFE

T/here

chalk bluffs
always there

two orange chairs
as usual

•

"maybe this is really a dream"

•

"all together with all the things together"

•

stream below cabin
chrrrrr of crickets at screen window
the child asleep at last

•

"Hi dad
'm making my bed"

•

All day
reading proofs
poolside

see the water
bugs

red
pen
tan
hand

sun
oak
shadow

clouds
blow
by

smooth
surface

SPLASH!

rip-
ples

read
"Riddles"

•

"Daddy
what are you
doing"

•

lifting stones
from the dam

to let steel–
head travel

•

gin
and
tonics

on the rocks

•

PINE
CONE
SPRING

water
crystal
analysis

parts per million
manganese
faint trace

mild laxatives
acid condition
sick headaches

catarrhal conditions
mucous membranes
urinary organs

Merritt 3733

•

"telephone wires
 go for miles"

•

PASSING CAR

gone

•

occasional plane
overhead

north to south
south to north

world beyond
BIG CANYON

•

funny family
up the road

Paula rescues
animals

leaves the kid to
her old man

Carl "you'll never
wake him up"

•

"get dressed go fishing"

•

strong tug
from rock

Water-
fall Pool

line, pink
-egg, hook

crayfish
should've been

snagged claw
drop it

•

"I almost catched the president lizard"

•

grass noose

•

random motion of
hundreds of dragonflies
FEEDING!

•

daddy-long-legs
making his way

across the wide
linoleum

•

"I love you best of all"

•

girl breaking glass
image of live oak

branches in blue pool
this last evening

•

"I won't die for a long long time"

TED BERRIGAN & TOM CLARK

from **Bolinas Eyewash**

The orange flower welcomes you to town. Bolinas. The hummingbird,
a piece of bumblebee stuck to its back—from the wind ! bids you all
too soon a farewell. Many things are current.

•

In the distance a blue lake gleams under purple mountains. A path
meanders, sheep graze. Tiny smoke creeps upward. In the hills a great
house nestles. It is the Hideum! Here our deepest fears reside. (We have
vowed to resolve them via committees.)

•

The word-of-mouth network plugs you in to what's happening inside
everybody else's houses, even if you never go there, & didn't want to.

•

Is the "it" in "don't worry about it" the same as the "it" in "take it
easy?" Or, if not the same, do both these terms derive their indelible
aptness from a common pump? These were my thoughts as I pulled
into Mr. Whitehead's filling station. Even thought it was well past 3
a.m. the silver-haired proprietor was waiting there alertly, hose in hand.

•

To get connected, plug yourself in, do this while turning & turning
around. Eat the sky-banana, let the silver turn gold & illuminate the
ground.

•

"We were first on the beach. The sets were rolling in at four to six,
with occasional eight footers. We waxed up and waited for a break."

•

Removing the trapdoor, I poke my head up far enough to inhale the
dusty muffler smoke of Venus. Out there, winter wants a bone to rip.
We'll throw it in the works to feed on instead. Stealing my spinal
power, holy shit!

•

Several surrounding communities are already considering regional
approaches to Open Space.

•

Eyelash transcript: Semi-permanent. You can wake up beautiful. Even
swim or cry. Call 868-9996.

•

8 Miles High, up here in the zone: mattress glitter & bodies that gleam
like stone weirdness: the golden fleece recumbently inclines in the
bread-like dawn: then decomposes slowly in the sun: like a hanky full
of fried chicken: & now I sense a strange perfume rising from this.

•

The earth's various surfaces are lovely. Many
float past me now. Further in, they collapse;
Dark/light emanations crash into my skull. Dove
and pearl grey skies melt into mussy blues, sickly electric
and flat black stars bob above like buoys, in bevies,
move. The sun's red ball tumbles into feathery depth.

•

The average Bolinas resident consumes or uses 75 gallons of fresh water
each day. Drinks Pepsi, takes shower, makes tea, washes feet, waters
cabbages, feeds goat, cat, wolf-dog killer pet, & 5 or more chickens.
Boils potatoes, shampoo, gets drunk on bud & washes hands many
times after pees. Combs hair & has huge drink of water after late
evening fuck scene in renovated Portuguese fishing shack beatnik-
hippie pad, surrounded by open books: A Separate Reality; Organic
Everything; How to Eat Well & Keep Fit; The Diamond Sutra; Zap
Comics; Blake's *Job*; & Dr. Spock. Then teenybopper daughter's horse
must drink, & toilet flush also uses more water. 75 gallons, probably
more even.

•

"I know you aren't afraid of bumblebees!"

•

I was born in 19 and 34 and I started learning the rules. I learned early
that the main thing was to be an ordinary man, that everything took off
from there (it was only much later I learned how many directions might
be contained in "took off.") JB told me that "Freedom is just another
word for nothing left to lose." I knew he was quoting JJ, but was more
concerned re: its validity as a rule. I'm thinking about it. JK (of Bolinas)

told me once, "Don't worry about it." This, I'd say, is the most relevant and therefore, e.g. not heavily, valid rule I had and have yet ever been quoted. You must reduce "it" to its most simple singular factor, and at that point the positive/negative quotient in proportion to direct application is, manifestly, & with all possible immediacy, *knowledge*, i.e., one's own, & there, of a kind Whitehead, with absolute impeccable aptness, speaks of as 'self-evident,' i.e. *true*. The only kind we want, too, buddy! But not the only kind you'll get, buddy! How true, how true.

•

The light gets more voltage. Strange birds make weird metallic noises. Tree-ferns rise. The fog moves in, throws a hip, head & shoulder fake, & reverses its field. Tonight, so late with a last desperate lunge, flops face forward into the mud-dust. The huge cheer of morning rises jubilant. I'm here. You still sleep.

•

Tom Sawyer painted Aunt Polly's house. God painted the sky. The Spanish Masters caught a golden light in that moment when autumn afternoon's sun-glow turns the corner and starts to run, flat-out, into evening's brown arms. There's a hint of winter in the air. "As Blue Turns to Grey," sing the Rolling Stones: wheels of pig-iron batter the roof. A penguin struts in, starkly garbed, out of German Expressionist movies of the 30s. Imagine the possibilities of being a stripe. But you can't always live in the sheer light of art. Not even for love.

•

The young deer dare to prance on the road & browse its grasses only when there's no traffic, so that most of the day they're off in the bushes, watching the future studies cars tool by, from concealed positions.

•

There's a track of light that races West off the reef to the horizon, holding late rays of the sun in chunks & patches. It's like a shimmering highway mirage on some incredible freeway through the Himalayas— built after due deliberation of the Emperor, by ten thousand impressed laborers, on each of whom it made a huge impression. It makes one on me, too: a Splendid Hue. The Golden Road to Unlimited Devotion! Light dancing from peak to peak across the Pacific, nimble past belief!

•

In our universe, the blinking of eyes is a great mystery, as the facts that are known up until now indicate. The lion blinks less than once a minute; some monkeys blink at an average of 45 times a minute. Blind people have normal blink rates. Humidity does not affect blink rates. In the blink, the upper lid closes like a window shade upon the lower lid, which temporarily goes "on the blink."

•

Moooooooo!   Arf!   Grrrrrrrrr!   *Grahr!*
                    Cock—a—doodle—doo!
Bolinas.
                    "The Daddy-Long-Legs capital of the West!"

(10 daddy longlegs a day fall, beneath the green sports pages of the San Francisco *Chronicle*.
                              But horrors! you kill the spiders & the houseflies wildly proliferate! Ugh!

Bzzzzzzzzzzzzzzzzzz-bzzzzzzzzzzzzz-bzzzzzzzzzzzzz & bzzzzzz.

"Buzz off you fucking fly, or it's the fly-paper scene for you!")

Bioled Vegtables.   Oreos.   Organic Meth.   Blue tea.   Sounds &
    Dreams in bed.   On the Mesa

all that's in my head.

•

NATURAL NUMBERS

TWO hummingbirds buzz in the fuchsias. It should be musical.
It should be light. SIX flounces a lot, THREE trills
FIVE loses itself in a noose of lilac stars
EIGHT gambols in moss where the soft, loose forest swarms.

NINE finds it hard to be easy, easy to be hard;
It plays its hand tight, holds all the best cards
Because it has extra lives; is tough; whereas ONE
Wears its hart on its sleeve, relies on bluffs,

Dies early. FOUR tells true stories, only half-admits
They are lies. SEVEN is unreal. It goes around & around
Like a mobile made of air. It's thrilled to be here.
It preens. It's as easy as it feels. Its hair

Falls across TEN'S sturdy shoulders. It is abstract,
It whispers. It makes you think a little local color
Might do you good; you feel a lack of that; you'd put
Some in right here, if you only could; you can, & do:

•

All of my friends are in another world.

•

Six months of each other for each of us began to evoke re-birth throes
Primitive magnetic expressions of the heads,
Above all the hypnotic presence of staring eyes that have a ritualistic
      fixity
Whose force-beams not only cut wildly across the broad arcs of daylight
Into a literal jungle of coarse energies,
But whose fury becomes the substitute for
Rigorous control of eye & intellect; so,
A penchant for the grotesque is hardly absent

                                      each perfect day.

•

I am not a machine nor a pseudo-soul magician . . . and I'm not cheap
                    labor . . .

•

BOLINAS

    get, in the complexity of the present
    responsible elements seething between
    impasto excitation & somber, subtly evoked grandeur.

•

Pampas grass on Elm, a man painting a stolen VW Bus black on Fern,
while in downtown Bolinas at this moment 185 homes & businesses,
Smiley's, Snarley's, Pepper's et al. are being served by rotting sewer
pipes. Each day 45,000 gallons of raw sewage (ugh) are discharged into

the channel at the mouth of Bolinas Lagoon. This is a bunch of shit, according to the Future Studies Institute.

.

Nothing but blue days, & then again Old
Golds, with flights of canvas clouds
& light pre-warmed by Dutch Masters
or else dusty, movie-ish & cold
with ocean winds & garden mildew;

Space itself shapes your pleasures;
but hot blood's scolded by memories
until sight fails completely and you/one
don't know where to turn; that's Time.

It's not easy, & you can't hold out
but you can last; & that's the past:

take it or leave it, or take it & go on.

Tapes hanging off the nose of the Muse get good mileage. For the Oriole
to live in, there's a leaf-colored room, full of Rhesus monkeys, tropical
fish. The Minnesota twins perform a flowery adagio of the Kinks
on instant replay . . .

.

She is getting into Other Scenes.

Can't I just play my tapes,
sans meaning, to the Ether?

A moon white as Greek plaster
rises over The Chinese Language School

near to Mecca. Tonight is cool,
blue. The bowl of light rotates like a mobile.

Necco wafers.

•

When truth throws up its translucent roosters onto the fountains of
eggnog,
He wants you to see right through them. Just behind them are massive
granite anguish shapes, humped over, feet on the ground, snout to the
earth.
If you want to see the light-show, touch that hump, you rooster!

•

The land, sprinkled with dwellings; like granola & granulated sugar:
it takes time to get behind it.

•

    Into the Valley of Death rode the 600
shouting,
        "Dig it!"

LEWIS MACADAMS

Eamon De Valera

Hey, I'd
love to sit here unfastening your safety belt forever,
but there's cows to push into the next pasture.

Last night I was nodding out until you showed me
a book you'd been reading about Du Chatelet.
She was Voltaire's mistress,
but she was this incredible scientist in her own right.
She looked a little like you actually,
from the frontispiece; & somehow we got to talking about journals,
and journalists, and you told me
I was a journalist.

What do you mean by journalist?

The tip of my tongue was numb
and my nose was frozen.

Well you wrote *Tilth* didn't you?

Yeah well, I guess you could call that
journalism,
in that it was written
with a particular future in mind,

a short future which has already passed,
and come true,
and that book helped make it come true.

              (She actually dressed up
            like the High Sierra last night.
      She cooked Halloween breakfast.
    And while I was with her
               my life veered back on track.)

    The man in the house

      the man of the house

One day later I'm sliding out of a rodeo.
in Kayenta, Arizona,

        if you can call that journalism
        There's a dust storm brewing.
        The gray wooden grandstands creak,
        and the silent Indian spectators watch the
        blond, hard, ultimately uptight cowboys
        try to hang on to bucking brahma bulls.
        One after another,
        the cowboys are flung to earth
        but nobody laughs.
        The arena's silent, but for the wind
        and whirr and click of lenses
        in the hands of black-suited
        Japanese tourist movie photographers
        who've come all this way
        to walk around inside
        their own parameters.

And what did you make of all this?

>Nothing. I just dug on it, for a while,
>then I hitched off down the road.
>Had to get out of there (too much dust). Had to
>Hitch off down the road.

>>The man in the house.

A little while later a man slides down the University Avenue on ramp,
and do you know who that man is?
Why it's Eamon De Valera.

It's funny.
>We could make love anywhere.
>At the warm rock pools
>>>by the Yuba River'd be groovy now
>>(the fog's rolling in)
>>>>while the children float by in tubes.

>>"Be" Refractures.
>>>Crystalline blue skies and pines
>>>>>as seen through
>>>a flurry of blow.

He's not gonna leave her.
He loves her.

The man in the house.
He's putting purple and white feathers around her bed,
but he's taken his woodpecker out for her.

The television's on. The chaise lounge is on.
                    Ommmmmmmmmmmmmm . . . . . .

Well, if I'm a journalist, then you're the Ideal Reader.
Someone I can meet late some nights but not others.
Someone I can talk to about books, and we can
get high and be together.
And your children are asleep we think,
          but actually
                    they're growing.
P.S. You know when to laugh, and you're indelibly kind.

                         And this is journalism,
                         on one level;
                         but it's not so simple.
                         It's complete.

               It's everything you see with
                    when you're walking down the street,
               say Mission Street, and it's 5 PM
               and you're coming off some psychedelic;
          Or you're getting off work, and hitting the neon
               for some sleep; or stopping at a record shop to cop
the new Freddy Fender 45.
Anything, just so it's hot and moving, you know?
I can feel the fire
moving down the street like a picture
of Eamon De Valera breathing into a packed meeting
of the Sinn Fein in nineteen eighteen,
                         and you're walking down the beach
in a long woolen coat and a purple scarf

and it's three hundred degrees Fahrenheit
and it's burning your toes it's so hot then your feet go up in smoke
and you're breathing in tears, you're crying so hard.
Your haunted orbs don't seem to see
the same things my haunted orbs see:
                    these peaceful animals,

                              lounging around
                    half-dressed or undressed,
                              I like them.
              I want to raise my children among them.
Why are you still hurting?

                                   "Well, if I don't
                                   see you anymore,
                                   may the good lord
                                   bless you everywhere you go,
                                   'cause it's
                                   bye-bye pretty baby,
                                   baby bye-bye."

                                   (A song Little Hat Jones was
                                        singing, circa 1930)

My Three Families

My three families
borrow the car
whenever they want to
(I'm falling asleep)
Blue money.

My family
totally blue
knows everything about love.

What is love,
and when did you last feel it
hurtle through your day?

What is love,
Hazarat
Inayat
Kahn?

Is it two pounds of pot?

A drive-in movie?

Unbelievable, bitter, literal

aching and longing
for my two sons,
all my thirty thousand thirsty thoughts
are not you.
We've been separated
for so many days and nights that
I don't know what to do
except love you fearlessly,
desperately lonely for you,
trying to cut through
the fantasy constantly
for me, and for you two too.
No other choice really,
but to be without you

a while longer. So
work hard scribbler.
Do your work. You can
live with this.

LAWRENCE KEARNEY

from **Songs**

flesh

the rough tunnel
its trees whistling
its low ripping off spray
        as it turns it

turns
it sleeps
it hits your thigh in the dark of a too short bed
feels your breathing
        not awake
to look
        not awake
to see
        not awake
to want
        not awake

for the reasons
of you
for the season
rain

for the sound the big windows in a dozen frames
dripping

between here and there
you don't wake up the earth
goes like hell
a planet
alone
I hit your thigh almost
in my sleep.

The hearts of cows
the big stupid eyes, the eye
of half awake is sleep

in an eye of love
beyond what is said what is just
need
not
sleeping touch sleeping sweet
flesh

edges of something alive the space
is full
cuts around the fertile edges
of leaves the redwoods

twirling
now
still up there
in the dark

the animals staring at night in the central park zoo
the apartment lights across the street
from the water buffalo
the camel
the seal pond, the empty terrace restaurant
the sweetness of aftermaths
twirling

sweetness
rolling

Mars and Venus
red and green
on either side Venus coming up with wide loins
and a belly like a hill
that smile
to touch awake or sleep the
green shine
green line
through the air into a flesh you think
is morning.

Where am I now, where
is that look of waking up
at night
and being
          annoyed
eyes full of charcoal waters
and seas full of long reptile necks and
days full of hissing and roaring

the sea foaming up at stars
the stars roaring
like hunters

the flesh of Venus
being fucked by the horizon, the curve
of coming
the loose neck
the please of it
let my legs go.

Charms.
        I don't know you.
Charms.
        I am in my bed I am
I am like the earth I am into
nothing
        twirling
every cell
in its own air.
Charms. I know
        how to kill
my ancestors knew how to kill
my ancestors died so know
how to,
this then shall be
this then was
this then shall be me dead you ded

the patches of ground
needing my flesh

212

the deep root trees
the ducks waddling down to the water
in my eyes

the green snake twisting heads
of plants

the tropics
the ice
the crackling sounds of ice hallways
the din feeling of legs
without moving
going down them singing
some song
some charm
some flash in the white water
on the ice.

There are other people
who are, all the time
other
in their heads

not me.

There are other people whose
mouths talk
whose
mouths talk

who spin too
who spin

lying in their beds.

The earth spins around the sun
which is tiny

fuller with the dark

than its light

I am a piece of a descent
can go faster
or slower
nowhere
or
nowhere
•
light
or dark
or light
or dark
or light
or dark
      or stop

at flesh
flesh
sweet flesh

just the feel of it
and knowing its speed
and tininess
and otherness one

of the people
not you
but you, one of you.

It's probably true
I care
more about the sky and leaves
walls

than people. Nothing is like it the flash

of solidarity in light

trees going by turning out of their flesh.

You walk down the road each
amaryllis
reflects.

I say
this is real this is true there
I am
walking
down the road.

Then there's a sense
of senses in a circle just
where they should be, that if

there's that real that bright
the haze and the clearness
have their real worlds their
invisible chested
blue plane people

walking past me like surfaces
the trees reflect in.

That once in a while
things are so bright and so deep
that it's worth it

more than that
just happening once

is worth everything.

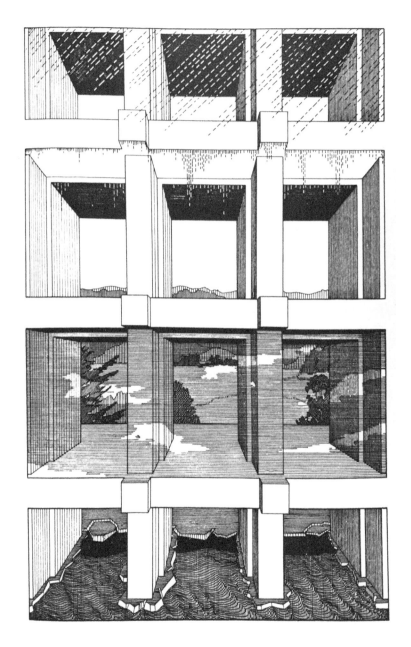

ALICE NOTLEY, TED BERRIGAN & TOM CLARK

Grain

a grain of sand

    •

you've gone from me
and left behind
a grain

    •

shoot half a grain
check to see what's left

    •

"which nevertheless could conjure up
a new"
grain:
       ease
            A mystery
          chooses my
      words

            A breeze

•

Flooded with joy

                    for one second

    in a world of pain & fear

              it's all OK
            going with the grain

•

In the American Grain

•

    we all shine on
    this tiny grain

•

in the Arabian grain the
octagonal grain the Sonnabend grain
the clarity grain the intricate
grain
         black stripes grain

•

now I don't know what I am saying and now
I do
    grain

•

A new bird swallows
     the grain
               it's gone
  we remain

    •

    Seen from Uranus

      The Earth

     a tiny green
          & blue grain

     going grey, grey

    •

I haven't a grain in my head
I haven't a grain in my hand

    •

But I have that feeling of absence
    of grain
         Plato calls "pain"

    •

I'd like to be secret-sharers with you
of the early morning grain
             which falls
into our hands from a heavenly source

    •

a girl could do better
than throw away her
hairs and grains

I mean "worse"!

I guess I did
                (grain, grain go away)

        •

in the cheap jokes grain
I feel no pain

        •

I'd like to see
"From Here To Eternity"
in the grain

        •

Familiar Grains

Familia
Granola
Semolina
Emily

        •

I have a horrible migraine headache on the moon
            in my dream
                    so I am allowed to

ride back to Earth

on Apollo 14

•

Thomas McGrane   pops up
        out of my 4th Grade class
            from the past.

•

He is grainier than the
grainy grain that grains
in early grain, mixed grain

•

Goodbye, grain. You were a new grain
        for us, so we went with you

until you were played out
        and we had a migraine
            from you, grain, o word

    mostly restricted to the products
            of agriculture
        until now, when we rescue you

            so goodnight
                & hello

•

a grain of prevention

was put to use

      but not before
    she had 9 babies

      •

a great drain

      •

We took you with a grain of salt
who became
a great Dane

      •

          mote in the eye

      •

grain, you are small
    but in your tiny bulk
    the poet, Blake

            found great
              wisdom

      •

   skin
   wood
   stone

all these things have grain

      •

Grain, you are engrained in me forever.

LEWIS WARSH

Part of My History

It's cold there, but
she's waiting up for me

& that's part of my history

Birthday Song

for Joanne

You can tell
how she's feeling
by the way she walks
how sad she must be feeling
it's the way she talks
how happy you wish she could be
when she's with you
you just don't know what she's thinking when she's gone

Her hair's light
brown her eyes don't
tear   she thinks
her feelings and her body doesn't care
for the cold
clear nights
when no one's
there   but
you don't know what she's thinking when she's there

Light brown hair
parts the air when
she's sleeping   trees
wear her clothing
like an empty chair
but when she talks they hear her spirit breathing
the air you're breathing
good feelings everywhere
and you don't want to know what she's thinking

In the Stars

Perhaps an evening awaits me
                                        when I will go
            peacefully
    to some small town
                            and settle down
                                there, for the
            life that awaits me

among the living
animals, and their effigies, the celestial forms

that light the way
                        down Elm Road
                                        towards home
            big
    empty house
                        filled with intimate thoughts
Perhaps that
evening you speak of
                            has already occurred
        so

        it is no longer necessary
    for anything to happen
                        but what you make happen

take the stars

and guide them across the road

or take the effigies of those thoughts
                    and write this poem

Definition of Great

Momentarily

          the language of description is lost

     what you see with your eyes is enough, for you, anyway

but how to get that sense of what you saw across

                    to another person

it's possible

        through the spirit in your voice

      when you say

        "it was great!"

to convey

        what happened
          in that moment

    & it was great

               not only that
    it was terrific, & interesting too

                it was nice

   & I had a good time doing it. I had fun.

You should have been there. Not only that, it was beautiful.
It was inspiring.

CHARLIE VERMONT

look to the light

over there

    here

and to the stranger

whoever comes
comes from
the other end of the sun

Red coals flicker
brighten the other corner

rearing high
over her ass
my mane tossing
the cold air
is everything
as I breathe in

One of these days
our sun
is going
to ZAP across
the night
sky
like a shooting star
some poet
in another solar system
will witness it
alone
thinking
about his wife
and the baby she carries

It's the Last Word

of

roses are red
violets are blue

you

me

    in the mountains
    and by the sea

    LOVE

    is the last word

Afterword

On the Mesa: Just Dropped In
(To See What Condition the Edition Is In)

Lytle Shaw

Beginning with the phrase "Chant's Operation," Tom Clark's poem "Inside the Dome of Taj Mahal" seems to use aleatory juxtapositions to disrupt the concentration necessary for a successful chanting session. Claims about the absorbing natural beauty of the site where the poem was written—Bolinas, California, a mesmerizingly gorgeous small town overlooking the Pacific Ocean on the south end of Point Reyes, north of San Francisco—emerge as a voice-over whose authority can't be trusted: "in nasal reef-voice, ah harmony / shimmering beyond choice." Though an active advocate of the community (Clark wrote numerous letters to friends encouraging them to visit or move to Bolinas), he could also poke some fun at life there. Before concluding with a recommendation about soundtracks perfect "if you just want to drift off and disappear," however, the poem also samples the line "the condition my condition was in," from the 1968 Mickey Newbury hit "Just Dropped In (To See What Condition My Condition Was In)."[1] Clark often incorporates rock

---

1. The song was first recorded by Newbury the year before; but it only became a hit when it was re-recorded and released by Kenny Rogers and the First Edition.

lyrics into his poems. This line, though, offers us a viable microcosm of the problems that confront us when we try to study the Bolinas community, the scene represented in *On the Mesa: An Anthology of Bolinas Writing*. Most of the poets who wound up there were coming down after a long decade of constant and often taxing activity: from full-on activism and small press publishing to around the clock socializing and grueling daily lives in cities that were seeming less and less livable—stress factors obviously varying poet to poet, whose involvement with activist politics (and with these other activities) also varied. Still, it is safe to say that the many poets who arrived in Bolinas from San Francisco, New York City, Buffalo, Albuquerque, and elsewhere were often, like the singer of "Just Dropped In," a bit dazed, badly overdue for scheduled maintenance—a "condition" indicated by the logical hiccup of the song's title.

But for those who missed the '60s themselves, "Just Dropped In" likely takes us back to the way they were framed by Hollywood in 1998, the year the song guided the bowling dream sequence of The Dude (Jeff Bridges) in *The Big Lebowski*. Here the song's quaint psychedelic ambiance becomes just further evidence of the Dude's delusional bad taste— like his bowling, his sweater and legging ensembles, his mumbling and, worst of all, his Students for Democratic Society past. Whatever slogan about "the system" or "change" a hippie student might have yelled in the heat of a rally, finally the '60s were about the process of becoming more attentive to "the condition" each private subject's "condition was in." As Bill Clinton continued the Reagan project of eviscerating the state, this was increasingly how '60s radicalism was coming to look to the practical realists of 1998, about when I began researching Bolinas.

Clark's poem was included in (but missed when I wrote about) the original *On the Mesa: An Anthology of Bolinas Writing*, edited in 1971 by Joel Weishaus. You are now holding in your hand the 50-year anniversary reissue of this anthology, edited by Ben Estes, which includes 66 new poems by 19 writers not in the original anthology. The importance of these numbers, and more importantly the careful selection behind them, is that they flesh out what was a fascinating if incomplete document into a more self-contained and usable picture of one of the great countercultural experiments of the later 20th century, the poet-run town of Bolinas. It is safe to say that most poets, literary scholars and even cultural historians remain unaware of exactly what American poets undertook in Bolinas. But imagine a city of about 500 people basically run by poets. No, it was not as dysfunctional as the image that just flashed into your brains: buildings aflame above monumental piles of uncollected garbage with a distant circle of hippies, unaware, out smoking weed on the nighttime beach. There were problems and conflicts, to be sure, but also a lot that transcended our received image of the '60s as an era simply about personal visions, indulgent drug use, and narcissistic and finally destructive attempts at self-care. Instead, poets in Bolinas sought to create an ecologically sustainable town where anyone could be an agent of news-making. Aware of their amazing natural resources—the views, the air, the sun, the northern Californian smells—they worked toward keeping these aspects of the town collective, and not privatizing it. They conceptualized poetry as a way to help focalize this present and its pleasures. And to do this the Bolinas poets also had to put some pressure on our familiar models of who gets to be a poet, and who a follower: while hierarchies wouldn't simply and finally disappear, the poets in Bolinas went quite a ways toward democratizing writing as a widely shared activity, and not only the province of isolated, revered stars—though there were some of these here as well. Poetry, we might say, wasn't just a shared interest among many of Bolinas' citizens; it was the organizing feature of daily life in the town, where most of the poets could survive on part-time, comparatively non-alienating jobs, or even on unemployment. Though it wasn't discussed much explicitly, we might see the attempt to reorganize time in places like Bolinas as part of a wider counterculture process of turning off or rejecting national time, with its labor/leisure division enforced by the work day and its building up of units of attention by the media, in particular the half hour and hour slots that were coming to rule so many American homes through television and radio.

The Bolinas attempt to put poetry at the center of this town was and wasn't singular. It emerged in part as a response to earlier American poetries of place, by which I mean not individual poems conceived of in relation to specific locations, but rather larger-scale projects that turned to place not merely for descriptive but also for social and historiographic purposes. I'm thinking in particular of what would have been for the Bolinas writers the two key American precedents, William Carlos Williams, and his *Paterson* (1946-1958, organized around the town in New Jersey,) and Charles Olson, and his *The Maximus Poems* (1953-1970), based on Gloucester, Massachusetts.[2] Both of these large, ambitious experimental poetry epics studied the histories of specific locations in order to trace out other, more capacious histories of the New World that might in turn sustain different kinds of social life, and social belonging, in the present. They were counter-nationalist epics. But the key difference between these two works and those undertaken by the wide range of poets in Bolinas is not only the diffusion of the singular project into that of an entire town; it was also that whereas for Williams and Olson the writing and research were directed toward readers in the future who might, they hoped, make good on their results, for the Bolinas poets there was an attempt to mobilize a place-based writing immediately—right now, in the present, and for themselves. As Clark put it, "No more rehearsals." In this sense Bolinas could be compared to a range of other attempts in the 1960s—all aligned with the New Left in various ways—to actual-

---

2. These dates cover the first publication of *The Maximus Poems* until Olson's death in 1970; the publication continued after his death, with the final volume coming out in 1983.

ize or enact place-based social formations. These would include Gary Snyder's familial compound in Kitkitdizze, where the poet designed a polemically extreme ecological structure for his family (no enclosure that would keep insects out, for instance) as a kind of essay about place-based living. They would also include Amiri Baraka's development of place-based living in Newark, after his moves—first from the downtown Manhattan Bohemian scene of the early 1960s to Harlem, and then from Harlem back to his hometown. There, Baraka was central in establishing Spirit House, a Black Nationalist collective that offered a complete re-education for African Americans, from food and clothing to music and poetry to politics and history.

By these standards the Bolinas experiment was not as thoroughgoing or organized, and no doubt would have been sneered at by many radicals in 1971, including Baraka, especially because his whole project involved a return to urban spots deemed unlivable and institutionally abandoned in part because the tax base was fleeing from the cities. From this angle Bolinas was part of the larger white flight phenomenon; the hippie community there was composed largely of white New Yorkers and San Franciscans who had found the cities unpleasant and had the means or contacts to escape. But the entire Bolinas project cannot just be dismissed in such broad sociological strokes—especially when popular culture urges us to be ungenerously impatient about such undertakings like this as well.

When I first started seriously researching late '60s poetry and Bolinas, I was drawn to it not just as an alternate community but as the only instance I could think of where a town was essentially governed by poets. That *so many* poets I was interested in were part of the experiment added another enticement. Bolinas seemed less like an important though undocumented moment in American poetry history than like a fantasy alternative history—one that hadn't *really* happened, but was fun and maybe even instructive to imagine. While *On the Mesa* was a point of departure, it was, as mentioned, an incomplete view: you simply couldn't understand the social dynamics of the place unless you read Joe Brainard's brilliant *Bolinas Journal*, for instance. Ted Berrigan's "Things To Do in Bolinas" also helped. Neither was included in the original anthology. Nor were Alice Notley, Bobbie Louise Hawkins, Duncan Mc Naughton, Aram Saroyan, Jim Brodey, Diane Di Prima, Philip Whalen, Anne Waldman, Phoebe MacAdams, Jim Carroll, Richard Brautigan, Gailyn Saroyan, Stephen Ratcliffe, Lewis MacAdams or Charlie Vermont. But all these poets had been there, and had written about it. I did not get to all of them during my own research—which involved a pretty crude (pre-easily searchable web) attempt to comb through period books from likely suspects and put the pieces together. So I all the more appreciate Ben Estes' thoroughness and care in adding these names and pieces of writing to our available Bolinas history—housing them conveniently as a new series of verandas on the original west coast bungalow of 1971. The writing I ultimately composed—"Non-Site Bolinas: Presence in the Poets' Polis"—was a chapter in my 2013 book *Fieldworks: From Place to Site in Postwar Poetics*. I won't try to replicate it here. Let me instead close by expressing optimism about both the simple fact of the reissue of this anthology, and the even more surprising expansion of what can now count as the Bolinas scene. This bodes well for those in the future, or right now, who would like to dive into actually thinking about both the counterculture and the poets' intimate ties to it. We have been offered more than enough tools for distancing ourselves from the '60s, for ironically undercutting "hippie" aspirations; it is therefore rare and wonderful to have an anthology like this placed before us—one that makes the past of 50 years ago look fresh and strange and attractive.

Bibliography/Permissions

Revolutionary Letters by Diane Di Prima, City Lights, 1971.

Own Your Body by Bobbie Louise Hawkins, Sparrow 15, Black Sparrow Press, 1973.

News from Niman Farm by Lewis MacAdams, Tombouctou, 1976.

Sunday by Phoebe MacAdams, Tombouctou 1983.

Sumeriana by Duncan Mc Naughton, Tombouctou, 1977.

Six Phoebe Poets by Alice Notley, unpublished, lent for publication by the author.

Grain by Alice Notley, Ted Berrigan, and Tom Clark, unpublished collaborative poem lent for publication by Alice Notley.

Drawings by Arthur Okamura, from the book *Sumeriana* by Duncan Mc Naughton, Tombouctou, 1977.

T/here by Stephen Ratcliffe, lent for publication by the author.

Day & Night: Bolinas Poems by Aram Saroyan, Black Sparrow Press, 1998.

Stories and Poems by Gailyn Saroyan, Tombouctou, 1977.

Two Women by Charlie Vermont, Angel Hair Books, 1971.

Spin Off by Anne Waldman, Big Sky books, 1972.

Eucalyptus by Joel Weishaus, uncollected, lent for publication by the author.

Severance Pay by Philip Whalen, Four Seasons Foundation, 1970.